LET US
DREAM

Center Point
Large Print

**This Large Print Book carries the
Seal of Approval of N.A.V.H.**

LET US DREAM

THE PATH TO A BETTER FUTURE

POPE FRANCIS

in conversation with Austen Ivereigh

CENTER POINT LARGE PRINT
THORNDIKE, MAINE

This Center Point Large Print edition
is published in the year 2021 by arrangement with
Simon & Schuster, Inc.

The text of this Large Print edition is unabridged.
In other aspects, this book may vary
from the original edition.
Printed in the United States of America
on permanent paper.
Set in 16-point Times New Roman type.

ISBN: 978-1-64358-832-2

The Library of Congress has cataloged this record
under Library of Congress Control Number: 2020950395

Contents

LET US
DREAM

Prologue

I see this time as a reckoning. I think of what Jesus tells Peter in Luke 22:31, that the devil wants him to be sifted like wheat. To enter into crisis is to be sifted. Your categories and ways of thinking get shaken up; your priorities and lifestyles are challenged. You cross a threshold, either by your own choice or by necessity, because there are crises, like the one we're going through, that you can't avoid.

The question is whether you're going to come through this crisis and if so, how. The basic rule of a crisis is that you don't come out of it the same. If you get through it, you come out better or worse, but never the same.

We are living a time of trial. The Bible talks of passing through fire to describe such trials, like a kiln testing the potter's handiwork (Sirach 27:5). The fact is that we are all tested in life. It's how we grow.

In the trials of life, you reveal your own heart: how solid it is, how merciful, how big or small. Normal times are like formal social situations: you never have to reveal yourself. You smile, you say the right things, and you come through unscathed, without ever having to show who you really are. But when you're in a crisis, it's the opposite. You have to choose. And in making your choice you reveal your heart.

Think of what happens in history. When people's hearts are tested they become aware of what has held them down. They also feel the presence of the Lord, who is faithful, and responds to the cry of His people. The encounter that follows allows a new future to open up.

Think of what we've seen during this Covid-19 crisis. All those martyrs: men and women who have laid down their lives in service to those most in need. Think of the health workers, the doctors and nurses and other caregivers, as well as the chaplains and all who chose to accompany others in their pain. Taking the necessary precautions, they sought to offer others support and consolation. They were witnesses to closeness and tenderness. Many, tragically, died. To honor their witness, and the suffering of so many, we have to build tomorrow by following the paths they have lit for us.

But—and I say this with pain and shame— let's also think of the usurers, the payday lenders who have appeared at the doors of desperate people. If they stretch out their hands, it is to offer loans that can never be repaid, and which end up permanently indebting those who accept them. Such lenders speculate with the suffering of others.

In moments of crisis you get both good and

bad: people reveal themselves as they are. Some spend themselves in the service of those in need, and some get rich off other people's need. Some move out to meet others—in new and creative ways, without leaving their houses—while some retreat behind defensive armor. The state of our hearts is exposed.

It's not just particular individuals who are tested, but entire peoples. Think of governments having to choose in the pandemic. What matters more: to take care of people or keep the financial system going? Do we look after people, or sacrifice them for the sake of the stock market? Do we put the machinery of wealth on hold, knowing people will suffer, yet that way we save lives? In some cases governments have tried to protect the economy first, maybe because they didn't understand the magnitude of the illness, or because they lacked the resources. Those governments have mortgaged their people. In making those choices, their priorities are tested and their values exposed.

In a crisis there's always the temptation to retreat. Of course there are times when we must pull back for tactical reasons—as the Bible says: "To your tents, O Israel!" (1 Kings 12:16)—but there are situations when it is neither right nor human to do so. Jesus makes that clear in his famous parable of the Good Samaritan. When the Levite and the priest withdraw from the man left bleeding and beaten by thieves, they're making a "functional" retreat, by which I mean they're trying to preserve their own place—their roles, their status quo—when faced with a crisis that tests them.

In a crisis, our functionalism is shaken loose and we have to revise and modify our roles and habits in order to emerge from the crisis as better people. A crisis always demands that our whole self be present; you can't retreat, pull back into old ways and roles. Think of the Samaritan: he stops, pulls up, acts, enters into the world of the wounded man, throws himself into the situation, into the other's suffering, and so creates a new future.

To act in a Samaritan way in a crisis means letting myself be struck by what I see, knowing that the suffering will change me. We Christians talk about this as *taking up and embracing the Cross*. Embracing the Cross, confident that what will come is new life, gives us the courage to stop lamenting and move out and serve others and so enable change, which will come only from compassion and service.

Some respond to the suffering of a crisis with a shrug. They say, "God made the world that way, that's just how it is." But such a response misinterprets God's creation as static, when it's a dynamic process. The world is always *being made*. Paul in his Letter to the Romans 8:22 says creation is groaning from birth pangs. God wants to bring forth the world with us, as partners, continually. He has invited us to join Him from the very beginning, in peaceful times and in times of crisis—at all times. It's not like we've been handed this thing all wrapped up and sealed: "Here, have the world."

In the Genesis account God commands Adam and Eve to be fruitful. Humankind has a mandate to change, to build, to master creation in the positive sense of creating from it and with it. So what is to come doesn't depend on some unseen mechanism, a future in which humanity is a passive spectator. No: we're protagonists, we're—if I can stretch the word—*co-creators*. When the Lord told us to go forth and multiply, to master the earth, he's saying: Be the creators of your future.

From this crisis we can come out better or worse. We can slide backward, or we can create something new. For now, what we need is the chance to change, to make space for the new thing we need. It's like God says to Isaiah: Come, let us talk this over. If you are ready to listen, we will have a great future. But if you refuse to listen, you'll be devoured by the sword (Isaiah 1:18–20).

There are so many swords that threaten to devour us.

The Covid crisis may seem special because

it affects most of humankind. But it is only special in how visible it is. There are a thousand other crises that are just as dire, but are just far enough from some of us that we can act as if they don't exist. Think, for example, of the wars scattered across different parts of the world; of the production and trade in weapons; of the hundreds of thousands of refugees fleeing poverty, hunger, and lack of opportunity; of climate change. These tragedies may seem distant from us, as part of the daily news that, sadly, fails to move us to change our agendas and priorities. But like the Covid crisis, they affect the whole of humanity.

Just look at the figures, what a nation spends on weapons, and your blood runs cold. Then compare those figures with UNICEF's statistics on how many children lack schooling and go to bed hungry, and you realize who pays the price for arms spending. In the first four months of this year, *3.7 million people died of hunger.* And how many have died from war? Arms spending destroys humanity. It is a very serious coronavirus, but because its victims are hidden from us we don't talk about it.

Similarly hidden to some is the destruction of the natural world. We thought it didn't affect us, because it was happening elsewhere. But suddenly we see it, we get it: a boat crosses the North Pole for the first time, and we realize the distant floods and forest fires are part of the same crisis that involves us all.

Look at us now: we put on face masks to protect ourselves and others from a virus we can't see. But what about all those other unseen viruses we need to protect ourselves from? How will we deal with the hidden pandemics of this world, the pandemics of hunger and violence and climate change?

If we are to come out of this crisis less selfish than we went in, we have to let ourselves be touched by others' pain. There's a line in Friedrich Hölderlin's *Hyperion* that speaks to me, about how the danger that threatens in a crisis is never total; there's always a way out. "Where the danger is, also grows the saving power."[1] That's the genius in the human story: there's always a way to escape destruction. Where humankind has to act is precisely there, in the threat itself; that's where the door opens. That line of Hölderlin's has been by my side at different points in my life.

This is a moment to dream big, to rethink our priorities—what we value, what we want, what we seek—and to commit to act in our daily life on what we have dreamed of. What I hear at this moment is similar to what Isaiah hears God saying through him: Come, let us talk this over. Let us dare to dream.

God asks us to dare to create something new. We cannot return to the false securities of the

15

political and economic systems we had before the crisis. We need economies that give to all access to the fruits of creation, to the basic needs of life: to land, lodging, and labor. We need a politics that can integrate and dialogue with the poor, the excluded, and the vulnerable, that gives people a say in the decisions that impact their lives. We need to slow down, take stock, and design better ways of living together on this earth.

It's a task for all of us, to which each one of us is invited. But it's a time especially for the restless of heart, that healthy restlessness that spurs us into action. Now, more than ever, what is revealed is the fallacy of making individualism the organizing principle of society. What will be our new principle?

We need a movement of people who know we need each other, who have a sense of responsibility to others and to the world. We need to proclaim that being kind, having faith, and working for the common good are great life goals that need courage and vigor; while glib superficiality and the mockery of ethics have done us no good. The modern era, which has developed equality and liberty with such determination, now needs to focus on fraternity with the same drive and tenacity to confront the challenges ahead. Fraternity will enable freedom and equality to take its rightful place in the symphony.

Millions of people have asked themselves and each other where they might find God in this crisis. What comes to my mind is the overflow. I'm thinking of great rivers that gently swell, so gradually that you hardly notice them, but then the moment comes, and they burst their banks and pour forth. In our society, God's mercy breaks out at such "overflow moments": bursting out, breaking the traditional confines that have kept so many people from what they deserve, shaking up our roles and our thinking. The overflow is to be found in the suffering that this crisis has revealed and the creative ways in which so many people have responded.

I see an overflow of mercy spilling out in our midst. Hearts have been tested. The crisis has called forth in some a new courage and compassion. Some have been sifted and have responded with the desire to reimagine our world; others have come to the aid of those in need in concrete ways that can transform our neighbor's suffering.

That fills me with hope that we might come out of this crisis better. But we have to see clearly, choose well, and act right.

Let's talk about how. Let's allow God's words to Isaiah to speak to us: *Come, let us talk this over. Let us dare to dream.*

PART ONE

A TIME TO SEE

In this past year of change and crisis, my mind and heart have overflowed with people. People I think of and pray for, and sometimes cry with: people with names and faces, people who died without saying goodbye to those they loved, families in difficulty, even going hungry, because there's no work.

Sometimes, when you think globally, you can be paralyzed: there are so many places of apparently ceaseless conflict, there's so much suffering and need. I find it helps to focus on concrete situations: you see faces looking for life and love in the reality of each person, of each people. You see hope written in the story of every nation, glorious because it's a story of sacrifice, of daily struggle, of lives broken in self-sacrifice. So rather than overwhelm you, it invites you to ponder, and to respond with hope.

You have to go to the edges of existence if you want to see the world as it is. I've always thought that the world looks clearer from the periphery, but in these last seven years as Pope, it has really hit home. You have to make for the margins to find a new future. When God wanted to regenerate creation, He chose to go to the margins—to places of sin and misery, of exclusion and suffering, of illness and solitude— because they were also places full of possibility:

21

"where sin increased, grace abounded all the more" (Romans 5:20).

But you can't go to the periphery in the abstract. I think often of persecuted peoples: the Rohingya, the poor Uighurs, the Yazidi—what ISIS did to them was truly cruel—or Christians in Egypt and Pakistan killed by bombs that went off while they prayed in church. I have a particular affection for the Rohingya people. The Rohingya are the most persecuted group on earth right now; insofar as I can, I try to be close to them. They are not Catholics or Christians, but they are our brothers and sisters, a poor people kicked from all sides who don't know where to turn. Right now in Bangladesh there are thousands of them in refugee camps with Covid-19 running riot. Imagine what happens when the virus hits a refugee camp. It's an injustice that cries to the heavens.

I met the Rohingya in 2017 in Dhaka: they are good people, people who want to work and take care of their families yet who are not allowed to, an entire population cornered and corralled. But what especially moves me is Bangladesh's fraternal generosity to them. It's a poor, densely populated nation; yet they opened their doors to 600,000 people. Their prime minister at the time told me how the Bangladeshis give up a meal each day so the Rohingya can eat. When last year, in Abu Dhabi, I was given an award—it was a significant sum—I had it sent straight to the Rohingya: a recognition of Muslims by other Muslims.

To go to the margins in a concrete way, as in this case, allows you to touch the suffering and the wants of a people but also allows you to support and encourage the potential alliances that are forming. The abstract paralyzes, but focusing on the concrete opens up possible paths.

This theme of helping others has stayed with me these past months. In lockdown I've often prayed for those who sought all means to save the lives of others while giving their own. I don't mean they were careless, or reckless; they didn't seek death, and did their best to avoid it, even if sometimes they couldn't because they had inadequate protection. But they did not prefer saving their own lives to saving others'. So many of the nurses, doctors, and caregivers paid that price of love, as did priests and religious and ordinary people whose vocation is service. We return their love by grieving for them, and honoring them.

Whether or not they were conscious of it, their choice testified to a belief: that it is better to live a shorter life serving others than a longer one resisting that call. That's why, in many countries, people stood at their windows or on their doorsteps to applaud them in gratitude and awe. They are the saints next door, who have awoken something important in our hearts, making credible once more what we desire to instill by our preaching.

They are the antibodies to the virus of indifference. They remind us that our lives are a gift and we grow by giving of ourselves: not preserving ourselves but losing ourselves in service.

What a sign of contradiction to the individualism and self-obsession and lack of solidarity that so dominate our wealthier societies! Could these caregivers, sadly gone from us now, be showing us the way we must now rebuild?

We are born, beloved creatures of our Creator, God of love, into a world that has lived long before us. We belong to God and to one another, and we are part of creation. And from this understanding, grasped by the heart, must flow our love for each other, a love not earned or bought because all we are and have is unearned gift.

How are we persuaded otherwise? How did we become blind to the preciousness of creation and the fragility of humanity? How did we forget the gifts of God and of each other? How to explain that we live in a world where nature is suffocated, where viruses spread like wildfire and bring down our societies, where heartbreaking poverty coexists with inconceivable wealth, where entire peoples like the Rohingya are consigned to the dustheap?

I believe that what has persuaded us is the myth of self-sufficiency, that whispering in our ears that the earth exists to be plundered; that others exist to meet our needs; that what we have earned or what we lack is what we deserve; that my reward is riches, even if that means that the fate of others will be poverty.

It is moments like these, when we feel a radical powerlessness that we cannot escape on our own, that we come to our senses and see the selfishness of the culture in which we are immersed, that denies the best of who we are. And if, at such moments, we repent, and look back to our Creator and to each other, we might remember the truth that God put in our hearts: that we belong to Him and to each other.

Perhaps because we have recovered, in lockdown, a little of that fraternity our hearts had painfully missed, many of us have begun to feel an impatient hope that maybe the world could be organized differently, to reflect that truth.

We have neglected and mistreated our ties with our Creator, with creation, and with our fellow creatures. But the good news is that an Ark awaits us to carry us to a new tomorrow. Covid-19 is our Noah moment, as long as we can find our way to the Ark of the ties that unite us: of love, and of a common belonging.

The Noah story in Genesis is not just about how God offered a path out of destruction, but about all that followed. The regeneration of human society meant a return to respecting limits, curbing the reckless pursuit of wealth and power, looking out for the poor and those living on the edges. The introduction of the Sabbath and the Jubilee—moments of recovery and reparation, forgiving debts and restoring relationships—were key to that regeneration, giving time for the earth to bounce back, for the poor to find fresh hope, for people to find their souls again.

That is the grace available to us now, the light in the midst of our tribulation. Let us not throw it away.

Sometimes, when I think about the challenges before us, I feel overwhelmed. But I'm never hopeless. We are accompanied. We are being sifted, yes, and it is painful; many of us feel powerless and even afraid. But there is also an opportunity in this crisis to come out better.

What the Lord asks of us today is a culture of service, not a throwaway culture. But we can't serve others unless we let their reality speak to us.

To go there, you have to open your eyes and let the suffering around you touch you, so that you hear the Spirit of God speaking to you from the margins. That's why I need to warn you about three disastrous ways of escaping reality that block growth and the connection with reality, and especially the action of the Holy Spirit. I'm thinking of narcissism, discouragement, and pessimism.

Narcissism takes you to the mirror to look at yourself, to center everything on you so that's all you see. You end up so in love with the image you created that you end up drowning in it. Then news is only good if it's good for you personally; and if the news is bad, it's because you are its chief victim.

Discouragement leads you to lament and complain about everything so that you no longer see what is around you nor what others offer you, only what you think you've lost. Discouragement leads to sadness in the spiritual life, which is a worm that gnaws away at you from the inside. Eventually it closes you in on yourself and you can't see anything beyond yourself.

And then there's *pessimism,* which is like a door you shut on the future and the new things it can hold; a door you refuse to open in case one day there'll be something new on your doorstep.

These are three ways that block you, paralyze you, and cause you to focus on those things that stop you from moving ahead. They are all in the end about preferring the illusions that mask reality rather than discovering all we might be able to achieve. They are siren voices that make you a stranger to yourself. To act against them, you have to commit to the small, concrete, positive actions you can take, whether you're sowing hope or working for justice.

One of my hopes for this crisis we are living is that we come back to contact with reality. We need to move from the virtual to the real, from the abstract to the concrete, from the adjective to the noun. There are so many real, "flesh-and-blood" brothers and sisters, people with names and faces, deprived in ways that we have not been able to see, listen to, or recognize because we have been so focused on ourselves. But now some of these blindfolds have fallen away, and we have a chance to see with new eyes.

The crisis has made visible the throwaway culture. The Covid health measures have exposed, for example, how many of our brothers and sisters do not have housing where social distancing is possible, nor clean water to wash. Think of so many families who live on top of each other in our cities, in the *villas miseria*, as in Argentina we call the slums and shantytowns, of so many places around the world. Think of the migrant holding centers and refugee camps where people can spend years unwelcome in any place, crammed together. Think of the way they are denied the most elemental rights: to hygiene, to food, to a dignified life, of how refugee camps turn dreams of a better life into torture chambers.

Talking to some shantytown priests during the pandemic, I asked them: How does a family in a shantytown observe social distancing to avoid contamination? How do they obey the health regulations without clean water? The crisis exposes these injustices. What will we do about them?

If Covid gets into a refugee camp it can create a real catastrophe. I'm thinking for example of the camps in Lesbos, which I visited in 2016 with my brothers Bartholomew and Ieronymos, and of films I've seen of the way migrants are exploited in Libya.[2] You have to ask: Is this drama just about Covid or is it also about what Covid has uncovered? Is this just a virus pandemic and an economic meltdown, or is it about widening our gaze, the way we take in all these human dramas?

Look at the U.N. statistics about the children without schooling in Africa, the children going hungry in Yemen, and many other tragic cases. Just look at the kids. It's clear that being stopped in our tracks by Covid has to make us think about all this. What worries me is that already there are plans afoot to restore the socioeconomic structure that preceded Covid, ignoring all those tragedies.

We have to find ways for those who have been cast aside to act, so that they become the agents of a new future. We have to involve people in a common project that doesn't just benefit the small number who govern and make decisions.

We have to change the way society itself operates in the wake of Covid.

When I speak of change I don't just mean that we have to take better care of this or that group of people. I mean that those people who are now on the edges become the protagonists of social change.

That's what's in my heart.

Let's consider a big obstacle to change, the existential myopia that allows us defensively to select what we see. Existential myopia is always about holding on to something we're afraid to let go of. Covid has unmasked the other pandemic, the virus of indifference, which is the result of constantly looking away, telling ourselves that because there is no immediate or magic solution, it is better not to feel anything.

We see it in the story of the poor man Lazarus in Luke's Gospel. The rich man was his neighbor; he knew perfectly well who Lazarus was—even his name. But he was indifferent, he didn't care. To the rich man, Lazarus's misfortune was his own affair. He probably said "Poor thing!" every time he passed him at the gate, peering at him over an abyss of indifference. He knew Lazarus's life but didn't let it affect him. This is what ends up creating a breach between the indifference that we feel on the one hand and our thoughts on the other. Hence people judge situations without empathy, without any ability to walk for a time in the other's shoes.

I saw a photography exhibition here in Rome. One of the photos was called just that: *Indifference*. A lady is leaving a restaurant in winter, well wrapped up against the cold: leather coat, hat, gloves, all the apparel of the well-to-do. At the door of the restaurant a woman is seated on a crate, poorly dressed, shivering in the street, holding out her hand to the lady, who looks elsewhere. That photo touched a lot of people.

Here in Italy you often hear people say *che me ne frega* when you have a problem. It means "So what? What's it got to do with me?" In Argentina we say: *y a mí qué*? They're little words that reveal a mindset. Some Italians claim you need a healthy dose of *menefreghismo*—"so-whatism"—to get through life, because if you start worrying about what you see, how are you ever going to relax? This attitude ends up armor-plating the soul; that is, indifference bulletproofs it, so that certain things just bounce off. One of the dangers of this indifference is that it can become normal, silently seeping into our lifestyles and value judgments. We cannot get used to indifference.

The attitude of the Lord is completely different, at the opposite pole. God is never indifferent. The essence of God is mercy, which is not just seeing and being moved but responding with action. God knows, feels, and comes running out to look for us. He doesn't just wait. Whenever in the world you have a response that is immediate, close, warm, and concerned, offering a response, that's where God's Spirit is present.

Indifference blocks the Spirit by closing us to the possibilities that God is waiting to offer us, possibilities that overflow our mental schemes and categories. Indifference doesn't let you feel the motions of the Spirit that this crisis must provoke in our hearts. It blocks the chance of discernment. The indifferent person is closed to the new things that God is offering us.

That's why we must become aware of this so-whatism and open ourselves to the blows that reach us now from every corner of the globe.

When that happens, we are flooded by doubts and questions: How to respond? What can we do? How can I help? What is God asking of us at this time?

And in asking these questions—not rhetorically, but silently, with attentive hearts, perhaps before a lit candle—we open ourselves to the action of the Spirit. We can start to discern, to see new possibilities, at least in the little things that surround us, or that we do each day. And then, as we commit to those small things, we start to imagine another way of living together, of serving our fellow beloved creatures. We can begin to dream of real change, change that is possible.

• • •

In these difficult times, I take hope from the last words of Jesus in Matthew's Gospel: "I am with you always, to the end of the age" (Matthew 28:20). We are not alone. That is why we need not be afraid to go down into the dark nights of problems and suffering. We know that we don't have the answers all ready and neatly packaged, yet we trust that the Lord will open for us doors we had no idea were there.

Of course, we hesitate. Faced with so much suffering, who does not balk? It is fine to tremble a little. Fear of the mission can, in fact, be a sign of the Holy Spirit. We feel, at once, both inadequate to the task and called to it. There is a warmth in our hearts that reassures us the Lord is asking us to follow Him.

When we face choices and contradictions, asking what God's will is opens us to unexpected possibilities. I describe these new possibilities as "overflow," because they often burst the banks of our thinking. Overflow happens when we humbly set before God the challenge we face, and ask for help. We call this "discernment of spirits," because it involves learning what is of God and what is seeking to frustrate His will.

To enter into discernment is to resist the urge to seek the apparent relief of an immediate decision, and instead be willing to hold different options before the Lord, waiting on that overflow. You consider reasons for and against, knowing Jesus is with you and for you. You feel inside yourself the gentle pull of the Spirit, and its opposite. And over time, in prayer and patience, in dialogue with others, you reach a solution, which is not a compromise but something else altogether.

I want to be clear about this. In the Christian life, when you're seeking God's will, there are no compromise solutions. Does this mean a Christian can never compromise? Of course not; sometimes it's the only thing you can do to avoid a war or some other calamity. But a compromise does not *resolve* a contradiction or a conflict. In other words, it's a temporary solution, a holding pattern, that allows a situation to mature to the point where it can be resolved by a path of discernment at the right time, seeking God's will.

In lockdown, the news and social media became our main windows onto the world, both for good and ill.

Journalists have had a key role in helping us to make sense of what was happening, to balance and assess different accounts and opinions. The best reporters took us to the margins, showed us what was happening there, and made us care. This is journalism at its most noble, helping us to conquer our existential myopia, and opening up spaces for discussion and debate. I want to pay tribute to the news media who in this crisis saved us from falling into indifference.

But the media also have their pathologies: disinformation, defamation, and a fascination with scandal. Some media are caught up in the post-truth culture, where facts matter much less than impact, seizing narratives as a way to wield power. The most corrupt media are those that pander to their readers and viewers, twisting the facts to suit their prejudices and fears.

Some media have used this crisis to persuade people that foreigners are to blame, that coronavirus is little more than a little bout of flu, that everything will soon return to what it was before, and that restrictions necessary for people's protection amount to an unjust demand of an interfering state. There are politicians who peddle these narratives for their own gain. But they could not succeed without some media creating and spreading them.

The media in this way cease to mediate and become intermediaries, obscuring our view of reality. Sadly, this phenomenon is not foreign to certain so-called Catholic media that claim to be saving the Church from itself. Reporting that rearranges the facts to support ideology for financial gain is a corruption of journalism that frays our social fabric.

In any case, as we have experienced personally in this time, no media can satisfy the human

35

soul's desire for direct contact with those they love and with reality; and nothing can substitute for engaging directly with the complexity of other people's experiences. Communication is much more than connection, and is most fruitful where there are bonds of trust: communion and fraternity and physical presence.

Social distancing is a necessary response to a pandemic, but it cannot last without eroding our humanity. We were born not just for connection but for contact.

It's risky to say this because I could be misunderstood, but the communication we most need is touch. Coronavirus has made us fearful about hugging and shaking hands with people. We yearn for the touch of those we love, which we must sometimes give up for their sake and ours. Touch is a deeply human need.

During Wednesday general audiences, when after giving a little teaching I went among the people, blind kids would say to me, "Can I see you?" and I would say, "Of course," without knowing at first what they meant. But then I realized they wanted to touch my face with their hands so they could "see" the Pope. Touch is the only sense that technology has yet to supplant. No device could allow those blind kids to "see" me as clearly as they did with their hands.

I've been so impressed with how so many in the

Church have responded to the pandemic, seeking new kinds of closeness to people while strictly observing social distancing measures: live-streaming liturgies, putting photos of members of their communities on pews, arranging meetings and prayers on digital platforms, giving remote retreats, contacting people by phone and tablet, making videos where dozens of singers and musicians contribute to a beautiful song from their homes. It has been a time, in the Church, of forced separation, yet also of new, creative ways to come together as the People of God.

Unable to celebrate Mass with their congregations, many priests went door-to-door, checking on their flocks through the windows, or exercising the apostolate of the telephone, in order not to lose that closeness with the people. Some did the shopping for self-isolating elderly people. In this time I have seen the Church alive; the witness has been extraordinary.

The internet has allowed us to be in contact and to communicate with each other but it has also changed the interior life of our lives and homes. Some have spoken to me of the effects of digital overexposure, of the exhaustion they have felt, of feeling invaded, of never finding relief—"living a life online" in every sense. Excessive exposure to screens is a new phenomenon that we should analyze carefully.

For example, social distancing has made some more vulnerable to online grooming and other kinds of abuse that as a community we should be watching out for and reporting.

In these past years, thank God, we have seen a particular awareness of these issues. The culture of abuse, whether sexual, or of power and conscience, began to be dismantled first by victims and their families, who, in spite of their pain, were able to carry through their struggle for justice and help alert and heal society of this perversity.

As I will not tire of saying with sorrow and shame, these abuses were also committed by some members of the Church. In these past years we have taken important steps to stamp out abuses and to engender a culture of care able to respond swiftly to accusations. Creating that culture will take time, but is an unavoidable commitment which we must make every effort to insist on. There must be no more abuse—whether sexual, or of power and conscience—either inside or outside of the Church.

We have seen this awakening also in society: in the #MeToo movement, in the many scandals around powerful politicians, media moguls, and businessmen. A mindset has been exposed: If they can have all they want, when they want it, why not take advantage sexually of vulnerable young women? The sins of the powerful are almost always sins of entitlement, committed by people whose lack of shame and brazen arrogance are stunning. In the Church, this sense of entitlement is the cancer of clericalism, as I call it, that perversion of the vocation to which we priests are called.

In these cases, the root of the sin is the same. It is the ancient sin of those who believe they have a right to own others, who recognize no limits, and, lacking all shame, believe they can use them as they wish. It is the sin of failing to respect the value of a person.

There is another abuse of power which we saw in the horrendous police killing of George Floyd that triggered protests around the world against racial injustice. It is right that people reclaim the dignity of every human being from abuse in all its forms. Abuse is a gross violation of human dignity that we cannot allow and which we must continue to struggle against.

And yet, such awakenings of consciousness, like all good things, run the risk of being manipulated and commercialized. I say this not to cast doubt on the many genuine and brave attempts to uncover the corruption of abuse and give the victims a voice, but to warn that sometimes we also find the bad within the good. I find it sad that there are lawyers who take advantage of abuse victims, not wanting to help and defend them but to profit from them.

The same can happen with politicians. I once received a letter from one who told me how in his country they had uncovered a whole history of abuse. A later investigation by judicial authorities discovered the accusation was untrue; the man was portraying himself as a hero for revealing abuse that had never happened. Later I found he wanted to be the governor of his state and was trying to use this to win votes.

To exploit, exaggerate, or distort a misfortune for political or social advantage is also a serious form of abuse that reveals contempt for the pain of victims. This, too, is to be deplored.

Some of the protests during the coronavirus crisis have brought to the fore an angry spirit of victimhood, but this time among people who are victims only in their own imagination: those who claim, for example, that being forced to wear a mask is an unwarranted imposition by the state, yet who forget or do not care about those who cannot rely, for example, on social security or who have lost their jobs.

With some exceptions, governments have made great efforts to put the well-being of their people first, acting decisively to protect health and to save lives. The exceptions have been some governments that shrugged off the painful evidence of mounting deaths with inevitable, grievous consequences. But most governments acted responsibly, imposing strict measures to contain the outbreak.

Yet some groups protested, refusing to keep their distance, marching against travel restrictions—as if measures that governments must impose for the good of their people constitute some kind of political assault on autonomy or personal freedom! Looking to the common good is much more than the sum of what is good for individuals. It means having a regard for all citizens, and seeking to respond effectively to the needs of the least fortunate.

We spoke earlier of narcissism, of armor-plated selves, of people who live off grievance, thinking only of themselves. It is the inability to see that we don't all have the same possibilities available to us. It is all too easy for some to take an idea—in this case, for example, personal freedom—and turn it into an ideology, creating a prism through which they judge everything.

You'll never find such people protesting the death of George Floyd, or joining a demonstration because there are shantytowns where children lack water or education, or because there are whole families who have lost their income. You won't find them protesting that the astonishing amounts spent on the arms trade could be used to feed the whole of the human race and school every child. On such matters they would never protest; they are incapable of moving outside of their own little world of interests.

Again, sadly, we cannot ignore those in our Church who fall into the same mindset. Some priests and laypeople have given a bad example, losing the sense of solidarity and fraternity with the rest of their brothers and sisters. They turned into a cultural battle what was in truth an effort to ensure the protection of life.

This crisis unmasks our vulnerability, exposes the false securities on which we had based our lives. It is a time for honest reflection, for owning our roots.

What worried me about the antiracist protests in the summer of 2020, when many statues of historical figures were toppled in several countries, was the desire to purify the past. Some wanted to project onto the past the history they would like to have now, which requires them to cancel what came before. But it should be the other way around. For there to be true history there must be memory, which demands that we acknowledge the paths already trod, even if they are shameful. Amputating history can make us lose our memory, which is one of the few remedies we have against repeating the mistakes of the past. A free people is a people that remembers, is able to own its history rather than deny it, and learns its best lessons.

In chapter 26 of the Book of Deuteronomy, Moses prescribed what the Israelites were to do after taking possession of the land the Lord had given them. They were to take the land's first fruits to the priest as an offering, and pronounce a prayer of gratitude that recalls the people's history. The prayer began: "A wandering Aramean was my ancestor." Then came a story of shame and redemption: how my ancestor went down into Egypt, lived as an alien and a slave, but his people called on the Lord's name and were brought out of Egypt, to this land.

The ignominy of our past, in other words, is part of what and who we are. I recall this history not to praise past oppressors but to honor the witness and greatness of soul of the oppressed. There is a great danger in remembering the guilt of others in order to proclaim my own innocence.

Of course, those who pulled down statues did so to draw attention to the wrongs of the past, and to deny honor to those who committed those wrongs. But when I judge the past through the lens of the present, seeking to purge the past of its shame, I risk committing other injustices, reducing a person's history to the wrong they did.

The past is always full of situations of shame: just read the genealogy of Jesus in the Gospels, which contains—as do all our families—quite a few characters who are hardly saints. Jesus does not reject his people or his history, but takes them up and teaches us to do likewise: not canceling the shame of the past but acknowledging it as it is.

Of course, statues have always come down and been replaced by others, when what they stand for no longer speaks to a new generation. But this should be done through consensus-building, by debate and dialogue rather than acts of force. That dialogue must aim to learn from the past, rather than judge it through the eyes of the present. Let's look at the past critically but with empathy, to understand why people took for granted what now seems to us abhorrent. And then, if we have to apologize for the mistakes made by institutions of that time, we can do so, but always keeping in mind the context of the time. It is not right to judge the past with the lens of today.

Just because it was justified then does not make it right then. But as humanity evolves, our moral consciousness develops. History is what was, not what we want it to have been, and when we try to throw an ideological blanket over it, we make it so much harder to see what in our present needs to change in order to move to a better future.

For a long time we carried on thinking we could be healthy in a world that was sick. But the crisis has brought home how important it is to work for a healthy world.

The world is God's gift to us. The biblical story of creation has a constant refrain: "And God saw that it was good" (Genesis 1:12). "Good" means bountiful, life-giving, and beautiful. Beauty is the entryway to ecological awareness. When I listen to Haydn's *The Creation*, I am transported into the glory of God in the beauty of created things. At the end, in the long duet of Adam and Eve, you meet a man and a woman enraptured by the beauty they have been given. Beauty, like creation itself, is pure gift, a sign of the God who overflows with love for us.

If someone who loves you gives you a beautiful and valuable gift, how do you handle it? To treat it with contempt is to treat the giver with contempt. If you value it, you admire it, look after it; you do not disdain it; you respect it and are grateful. The damage to our planet stems from the loss of this awareness of gratitude. We have grown used to owning, but too little to thanking.

My own awareness of this truth began to take root during a meeting of the bishops of Latin America at the shrine of Aparecida, Brazil, in May 2007. I was on the committee drafting the concluding document of the meeting, and at first I was a bit annoyed that the Brazilians and bishops from other countries wanted so much in there on Amazonia. It struck me as excessive.

Last year, I called a special synod on Amazonia. What had happened between these two moments? After Aparecida, I started to see news stories: for example, the government of a well-known island in the South Pacific bought lands in Samoa to transfer its population there, because in twenty years' time the island will be underwater. Another day, a missionary in the Pacific told me of when he was traveling by boat and saw a tree sticking up from the water. He asked: Was that tree planted in the sea? The man steering the boat told him: No, that was once an island.

And so, through many encounters, dialogues, and anecdotes like these my eyes were opened. It was like an awakening. In the night you see nothing, but little by little dawn breaks and you see the day. That was my process: serene and calm, through information I gradually became aware of, until I became convinced of the seriousness of the thing. What was particularly helpful were the writings of the Patriarch Bartholomew on this topic. It was a concern that I began to talk about to others, which helped. In sharing concerns, we began to see horizons and limits.

That's how my ecological awareness came about. I saw that it was of God, because it was a spiritual experience of the sort Saint Ignatius describes as like drops on a sponge: gentle, silent, but insistent. Slowly, like daybreak, an ecological vision began growing. I started to see the harmonious unity of humanity and nature, and how humanity's fate is inseparably bound up with that of our common home.

It's an awareness, not an ideology. There are green movements that turn the ecological experience into ideology, but ecological awareness is just that: awareness, not ideology. It's being conscious of what's at stake in the fate of humanity.

After my election as Pope I asked experts on climate and environmental science to assemble the best available data on the state of our planet. Then I asked some theologians to reflect on that data, in dialogue with experts in the field from across the world. Theologians and scientists put their heads together until they reached a synthesis.

While this was being worked on, in 2014, I went to Strasbourg in France to address the Council of Europe. President François Hollande sent his environment minister, who was at that time Ségolène Royal, to receive me. While we chatted at the airport, she said she had learned I was preparing an encyclical letter on care of the environment. I told her about it, and she said to please publish it before the meeting of heads of state that was due to take place in Paris in December 2015.[3] She wanted that meeting to turn out well. And it did, even though some later took fright and withdrew their support for its conclusions. It is important that the Church makes its voice heard in this vital, necessary process: our faith demands it.

Laudato Si' is not a green encyclical. It's a social encyclical. The green and the social go hand in hand. The fate of creation is tied to the fate of all humanity. When I give audiences in Saint Peter's Square, I greet the three or four rows of sick people who are there. Particularly in the case of the children, I ask: "What does he or she have?" I would say about 40 percent of the time it's "unusual sicknesses" caused by some neglect of the environment: the irresponsible use of waste, the reckless deployment of pesticides that are continually being developed. All these things, among others, end up making people ill and mortgaging the future of the generations to come. Often the doctors just don't know how to treat these illnesses. If it's an unusual sickness they have a fair idea where it comes from, but because it doesn't affect a large number of sufferers, it's not profitable for the laboratories to develop medicines.

You can't eat an apple these days without peeling it first in case it does you harm. Doctors advise mothers not to give their kids chicken from factory farms until they're four years old, because the chickens have been fattened with hormones that can make the kids unbalanced.

So this is not an ideological thing. It's a

dangerous reality. Humanity is getting ever sicker along with our common home, with our environment, with creation.

A year ago I met fishermen from the Italian town of San Benedetto del Tronto who told me of the tons of plastic they had fished up from the sea. Theirs is a fleet of small boats, crews of no more than maybe six or seven on board each one. This year they came to see me again and told me they had hauled up twenty-four tons of garbage of which about half—that's twelve tons—was plastic. They've taken it upon themselves as a kind of mission not to throw it back in the water. So along with the fish, they gather the plastic and separate it on the boats—which costs money, of course.

Laudato Si' links the scientific consensus on the destruction of the environment with our self-forgetting, our rejection of who we are as creatures of a loving Creator, living inside His creation but at odds with it. It's the sadness of a humanity rich in know-how but lacking the inner security of knowing ourselves as creatures of God's love, a knowledge expressed in our simultaneous respect for God, for each other, and for creation.

To talk about creation, you need poetry and beauty. Along with beauty is harmony, the sense of harmony that we abandon when we narrow our focus onto some areas at the expense of others.

Existence becomes lopsided when we focus on the technical and the abstract and lose our roots in the natural world. When we neglect Mother Earth we lose not just what we need to survive but the wisdom to live together well.

A humanity impatient with the limits that nature teaches is a humanity that has failed to master the power of technology. In other words, technology has ceased to be our instrument and has become our overlord. It has changed our mindset. How? We become more intolerant of limits: if it can be done, and it is profitable, we see no reason why it shouldn't be done. We begin to believe in power, confusing it with progress, such that whatever boosts our control is seen as beneficial.

Our sin lies in failing to recognize value, in wanting to possess and exploit that which we do not value as a gift. Sin always has this same root of possessiveness, of enrichment at the expense of other people and creation itself. It's the same sinful mindset that we were just discussing in relation to abuse. The sin is in exploiting what must not be exploited, in extracting wealth (power or satisfaction) from where it should not be taken. Sin is a rejection of the limits that love requires.

That's why I spoke in *Laudato Si'* of a distorted mindset known as the "technocratic paradigm." It is a mindset that despises the limit that another's value imposes. I made the case there that an ecological conversion is necessary to save humanity not only from destroying nature but from destroying itself. I called for an "integral ecology," an ecology that is about much more than caring for nature; it's about caring for each other as fellow creatures of a loving God, and all that this implies.

In other words, if you think abortion, euthanasia, and the death penalty are acceptable, your heart will find it hard to care about the contamination of rivers and the destruction of the rainforest. And the reverse is also true. So even while people will argue strenuously that these issues are different in moral terms, as long as they insist that abortion is justified but not desertification, or that euthanasia is wrong but polluted rivers are the price to pay for economic progress, we will remain stuck in the same lack of integrity that put us where we are now.

I think Covid-19 is making this apparent, for those with eyes to see. This is a time for integrity, for exposing the selective morality of ideology, and for embracing the full implications of what it means to be children of God. That is why I think the future we are called to build has to begin with an integral ecology, an ecology that takes seriously the cultural and ethical deterioration that goes hand in hand with our ecological crisis. The individualism brought on by the technocratic paradigm has its consequences.

• • •

Any disruption to our daily lives releases a great number of feelings and reactions. In some cases lockdown led to an increase in domestic violence because many people don't know how to live together. There was a notable increase in aggression, in sexual and physical abuse—very painful things. But in other cases, lockdown brought to the surface fraternal feelings that strengthened bonds. Parents could play more with their children, husbands and wives could discuss matters in new depth.

A "stoppage" can always be a good time for sifting, for reviewing the past, for remembering with gratitude who we are, what we have been given, and where we have gone astray.

These are moments in life that can be ripe for change and conversion. Each of us has had their own "stoppage," or if we haven't yet, we will someday: illness, the failure of a marriage or a business, some great disappointment or betrayal. As in the Covid lockdown, those moments generate a tension, a crisis that reveals what is in our hearts.

At such moments, we need others to walk with us. Some of us are allergic to doctors, but if you want to avoid unnecessary suffering or even the risk of a worse pain or illness, you need to seek guidance. The same is true when you're suffering an internal or personal crisis; you need to find people who are wise, who have been through the fire, people who can help you navigate what is to come.

In every personal "Covid," so to speak, in every "stoppage," what is revealed is what needs to change: our lack of internal freedom, the idols we have been serving, the ideologies we have tried to live by, the relationships we have neglected. What is the greatest fruit of a personal Covid? I'd say patience, sprinkled with a healthy sense of humor, which allows us to endure and make space for change to happen.

Two biblical characters come to mind whose "Covid" stories can help us understand our own. First, the Covid of Saul/Paul. Think of what happened to this fighter, full of zeal and ideals. Incensed by the deformation of Judaism that Jesus's disciples were bringing about, he was determined to crush them. He was filled with utter certainty and clarity when he was confronted with an event that inverted all his priorities.

His encounter with Christ threw him on the ground; he was blinded, and everything changed. He no longer lived for an idea, but for the person he recognized as the Lord. But while the switch was sudden, it took time to work through. He accepted help, allowed himself to be purified, went to Arabia, and eventually, after fourteen years, began to speak to the apostles as the one we know as Paul. It is striking how, in the Bible, these processes go hand in hand with a change in name; they are processes that forge a new identity: from Saul to Paul.

King David had three powerful moments of rupture and crisis, his own Covids. First, he tried to resolve his adultery with an appalling crime—he ordered the death of Uriah, Bathsheba's husband—but eventually, when he saw the wrong he had done, he repented. He got up again, started over. But then came his second Covid, when pride and self-sufficiency took over; rather than trusting God, he sought to increase his power over the population by taking a census. Later he repented, begged for compassion for his people, saying to God, in effect, "Punish me instead, these people are innocent."

Finally there was the Covid of David's flight, when he was betrayed by his son Absalom and forced to flee Jerusalem. Shimei curses and throws stones at David, and one of his generals says, "Why should this dead dog curse my lord the king? Let me go over and cut off his head" (2 Samuel 16:9), but David tells him not to, saying, "Let him alone, and let him curse; for the Lord has bidden him" (2 Samuel 16:11). David humbles himself.

These biblical stories we share show us that crisis is a time of purification. They all bring us to the same place, to a shaming of our arrogance and a trusting in God.

Two other "Covid" stories from the Bible come to mind, in which the crisis arises not from sin or misfortune but from neglecting a gift. That's what happens to Solomon and Samson. Both receive a great gift: Solomon is given the immense wisdom he asked for, while Samson gets the vast strength he needs to fight his enemies. But both end badly because they did not honor their gifts.

Solomon was an immense success, the wisest, richest man of his time. The Queen of Sheba said she had never seen such a well-organized palace: such amazing banquets and splendid clothes! His really was a world-renowned, first-class operation. But she was also struck by Solomon's great wisdom. He had asked God for the gift of discernment and that's what he had. Hence, the famous story of his judgment of the two women who claim to be the mother of the same child. All of Israel was amazed by the wisdom God had given Solomon.

But his heart grew cold as his ego expanded, and he became self-indulgent, as if what he had been given he deserved. He became lax in everything, but especially in the one area you really can't be lax about: worship of God, the source of his gifts. Saint Gregory the Great described this fall from grace in his *Morals on the Book of Job*. When a weak person receives a lot of praise, said Gregory, he "does not so much delight to *become* as to be *called* blessed," and gradually, in seeking after applause, he "is severed from God by the same means by which it appeared to be commendable in God."[4]

Solomon ends badly, surrounded by enemies, his kingdom divided, a pitiful man. And it's essentially the same with Samson: an incredibly strong man with a fatal weakness, who lets himself be seduced, and is captured after he lets slip to Delilah his secret and she betrays him. But in time he recovers his strength and identity, remakes his life of fidelity to God, and ends with a heroic act. There is life after a crisis, after Covid.

The Covids of Solomon and Samson are a positive kind of "stoppage," because it rescues us from worldliness, from an egotistic self-satisfaction, from *benessere* as they say in Italy. Self-indulgent living brings sterility. The demographic winter many Western countries are now living through is the fruit of that complacent culture of selfish well-being. It's hard for people to understand how *benessere*, which seems like a desirable thing, should be the state we desperately need to be rescued from. But that's one of the main lessons we can take from the fates of Solomon and Samson.

I've experienced three "Covids" in my own life: my illness, Germany, and Córdoba.

When I got really sick at the age of twenty-one I had my first experience of limit, of pain and loneliness. It changed the way I saw life. For months, I didn't know who I was, and whether I would live or die. The doctors had no idea whether I'd make it either. I remember hugging my mother and saying: "Just tell me if I'm going to die." I was in the second year of training for the priesthood in the diocesan seminary of Buenos Aires.

I remember the date: August 13, 1957. I got taken to hospital by a prefect who realized mine was not the kind of flu you treat with aspirin. Straightaway they took a liter and a half of water out of the lung, and I remained there fighting for my life. The following November they operated to take out the upper right lobe of one of the lungs. I have some sense of how people with coronavirus feel as they struggle to breathe on ventilators.

I remember especially two nurses from this time. One was the senior ward matron, a Dominican sister who had been a teacher in Athens before being sent to Buenos Aires. I learned later that, following the first examination by the doctor, after he left she told the nurses to double the dose of medication—basically penicillin and streptomycin—he had prescribed, because she knew from experience I was dying. Sister Cornelia Caraglio saved my life. Because of her regular contact with sick people, she understood better than the doctor what they needed, and she had the courage to act on her knowledge.

Another nurse, Micaela, did the same when I was in intense pain, secretly prescribing me extra doses of painkillers outside my due times. Cornelia and Micaela are in heaven now, but I'll always owe them so much. They fought for me to the end, till my eventual recovery. They taught me what it is to use science but also to know when to go beyond it to meet particular needs.

I learned something else from that experience, which is the importance of avoiding cheap consolations. People came in to tell me I was going to be fine, how with all that pain I'd never have to suffer again—really dumb things, empty words, said with good intentions but which never reached my heart. The one who spoke most deeply to me, with her silence, was one of the women who marked my life, Sister María Dolores Tortolo, who had taught me as a child, and prepared me for my First Communion. She came to see me, took my hand, gave me a kiss, said nothing for a while, and then eventually told me: "You're imitating Jesus." She didn't need to say more. Her presence, her silence, was deeply consoling.

After that experience I made the decision, when visiting the sick, to speak as little as possible. I just hold their hands.

The serious illness I lived through taught me to depend on the goodness and wisdom of others. Fellow seminarians came to donate their blood, to visit me and be with me; one used to sit by my bed, night after night, in that difficult situation. These are things you don't forget. How did I come out of this "Covid"? Better, more realistic. It allowed me the space to rethink my vocation. I was already feeling that my calling was to religious life, and was thinking about the Salesians, the Dominicans, maybe the Jesuits. I first met the Jesuits in seminary, because they ran it, and I was impressed by their missionary commitment. While recovering from my lung operation away from the seminary I had the space and time to ponder all this, and to reach the peace I needed to make a definitive decision to join the Society of Jesus (Jesuits).

My time in Germany in 1986 one might call "the Covid of displacement." It was a voluntary uprooting because I went to improve my German and seek material for my thesis, but I felt like a square peg in a round hole. I used to walk over to the cemetery in Frankfurt and from there watch planes land and take off, pining for my homeland. I remember the day when Argentina won the World Cup. I didn't watch the match and realized we had won the next day only when I read the papers. I got to my German class and no one said a word, but then a Japanese girl got up and wrote VIVA ARGENTINA on the blackboard and everyone burst out laughing. The teacher came in, told her to erase it, and that was that.

It was the loneliness of a triumph you can't share, the solitude of nonbelonging, of being thrown off balance. You're taken from where you are and sent to where you do not know, and in the process you learn what really matters in the place you left behind.

Sometimes the uprooting can be a healing or a radical makeover. That was my third Covid, when I was sent to Córdoba between 1990 and 1992. This time had its roots in my way of exercising leadership, as provincial and then rector. I'm sure I did a few good things, but I could be very harsh. In Córdoba they made me pay and they were right to do so.[5]

I spent a year, ten months, and thirteen days in the Jesuit residence there. I celebrated Mass, heard confessions, and gave spiritual direction but hardly ever left the house, just to go to the post office. It was a kind of lockdown, self-isolating as so many of us have done lately, and it did me good. It helped me to develop ideas: I wrote and prayed a lot.

Until then I had led an ordered existence in the Society of Jesus based on my experience of leadership, first as novicemaster and then, from 1973, when I was named provincial, through to 1986, when I ended my term as rector. I was settled into that way of life. So an uprooting of that kind, when they send you off the soccer field and put you on the bench, turns everything around. Your habits, your reflexive behaviors, the reference points of your existence that take shape over time—all these get turned on their head, and you have to learn to live life anew, to take up arms again.

Looking back now, I'm struck by three things in particular. First, the capacity for prayer I was given. Second, the temptations I experienced. And third—weirdest of all—why it occurred to me to read all thirty-seven volumes of Ludwig Pastor's *History of the Popes*. I could have read a novel, or something more interesting. But from where I am now I can't help wondering why God inspired me to read them. It was as if the Lord was preparing me with a vaccine. Once you know that papal history, there's not much that goes on in the Vatican curia and the Church today that can shock you. It's been a lot of use to me!

The Covid of Córdoba was a real purification. It gave me greater tolerance, understanding, the ability to forgive, and a fresh empathy for the powerless. And patience: a lot of patience, which is the gift of understanding that important things need time, that change is organic, that there are limits and we have to work within them while keeping our eyes on the horizon, as Jesus did. I learned the importance of seeing the big in little things, and attending to the little in big things. It was a period of growth in many ways, the kind of new growth that happens after a harsh pruning.

But I must still be vigilant, because when you fall into certain defects, into particular patterns of sinfulness, and you correct yourself, the devil comes, as Jesus says, and, finding the house "swept and put in order" (Luke 11:25), sends seven other spirits even worse. This man's end, says Jesus, is a lot worse than his beginning. That's what I must guard against in my work of governing the Church, that I don't fall back into the defects I had when I was a religious superior.

This "second tempting" is the speciality of polite demons. When Jesus says the devil sends seven demons worse than him, he says they "enter and live there." In other words, we let them in. They ring the bell, they're courteous, they say "Excuse me" and "May I?" but they take over the house just the same. It's the temptation of the devil in the guise of an angel of light that Jesus shows us in these passages.[6]

The devil's return in the form of temptation is a long tradition in the Church. Think of the temptations of Saint Anthony, for example, or Saint Thérèse of Lisieux asking to have holy water thrown over her because the devil is surrounding her, hoping she'll trip up eventually. At my age, I should have special glasses to see when the devil is surrounding me, hoping I'll trip up at the end, because that's where I am: I'm at the end of my life.

These were my main personal Covids. What I learned was that you suffer a lot, but if you allow it to change you, you come out better. But if you dig in, you come out worse.

Right now I see a lot of digging in. The people most invested in the current way of doing things are doing just that. There are leaders talking about making a few adjustments here and there, but they're basically advocating for the same system as before. When they talk of "recovery" they mean putting a bit of varnish on the future, touching up the paintwork here and there, but all to make sure that nothing changes. I'm convinced that this will lead to an even greater failure, one that could ignite a huge social explosion.

Something similar happened after the financial crisis of 2008 when governments spent billions of dollars rescuing the banks and financial markets, and the people had to endure a decade of austerity. This time we can't make the same mistake. If the choice is between saving lives and saving the financial system, which will we choose? And if we go ahead now into a world recession, will we adapt the economy to the needs of the people and creation, or will we continue to sacrifice these to keep the status quo?

For me it's clear: we must redesign the

economy so that it can offer every person access to a dignified existence while protecting and regenerating the natural world.

What I also see—and this gives me hope— is a people's movement calling for profound change, a change that flows from the roots, from the concrete needs of people, that arises from the dignity and the freedom of the people. This is the deep change we need, change that arises from people capable of meeting, organizing, and coming up with truly human proposals.

The Book of Nehemiah comes to mind. Nehemiah feels a call to remake Jerusalem, and he convinces his people. And the people rise up against the unbelievers who rule over them, and even those who are making war on them. In the fourth chapter there's a verse that describes how some worked at building the wall while others acted as guards to protect them, and how "each labored on the work with one hand and with the other held a weapon" (4:17). In other words, they knew they had to defend their future from falling back into the previous tragedy.

The first eight chapters in particular of the Book of Nehemiah can shed a lot of light for us right now: the whole struggle on behalf of the poor and restoring people's dignity, right up to the joy of achieving what they set out to do. It's a joy that brings the people to tears as they listen to the Book of the Law that had been recovered, at the end of which Nehemiah tells them to go to their homes and feast. Don't be sad, he says, "for the joy of the Lord is your strength" (8:10). That joy gives us the strength to move forward.

Today our peoples lack joy: there is a sadness that no pleasure or distraction can relieve. As long as one part of humanity is suffering the most abject misery, how can any of us be joyful? But at the same time we see an awakening, a call for change, a sense that what has been is not all there is to come. The joy of the Lord is their strength, but they know they have a road ahead before they can eat, drink, and rejoice in the new way of living.

Today we have to avoid falling back into the individual and institutional patterns that have led to Covid and the various crises that surround it: the hyperinflation of the individual combined with weak institutions and the despotic control of the economy by a very few. I see, above all, the pressing need to strengthen institutions, which are a vital reserve of moral energy and civic love.

Of all the institutions, the family has taken the hardest knock of all. It has lost or at least blurred its social identity as the "first society," where the person is formed as a member of something larger, with rights and duties and security. To erode the family is to fatally weaken the bonds of belonging on which we all depend. You can see this in the tragedy of young and old isolated from each other. It's an intuition, but I've long believed that if we pay attention to both of these groups, bring them in from the outside and bring them together, great things will happen.

The hyperinflation of the individual goes along with the weakness of the state. Once people lose a sense of the common good, history shows that we are left with anarchy or authoritarianism or both together: a violent, unstable society. We are there already: just consider the numbers of people who die each year from gun violence in the Americas. Since the outbreak of the crisis in the United States, sales of guns have broken all records.

Without the "we" of a people, of a family, of institutions, of a society that transcends the "I" of individual interests, life quickly fractures and becomes violent, a battle for supremacy between factions and interests; and if the state is no longer capable of managing violence for the sake of social peace, it can end up fomenting violence to defend its interests.

We are not there yet. This crisis has called forth the sense that we need each other, that the people still exists. Now is the time for a new Nehemiah project, a new humanism that can harness this eruption of fraternity, to put an end to the globalization of indifference and the hyperinflation of the individual. We need to feel again that we need each other, that we have a responsibility for others, including for those not yet born and for those not yet deemed to be citizens.

We can reorganize the way we live together in order better to choose what matters. We can work together to achieve it. We can learn what takes us forward, and what sets us back. We can choose.

PART TWO

A TIME TO CHOOSE

B etween the first step, which is to come close and allow yourself to be struck by what you see, and the third step, which is to act concretely to heal and repair, there is an essential intermediate stage: to discern, and to choose. A time of trial is always a time of distinguishing the paths of the good that lead to the future from other paths that lead nowhere or backward. With clarity, we can better choose the first.

For this second step, we need not just openness to reality but a robust set of criteria to guide us: knowing we are loved by God, called to be a people in service and solidarity. We need, too, a healthy capacity for silent reflection, places of refuge from the tyranny of the urgent. Most of all, we need prayer, to hear the prompts of the Spirit and cultivate dialogue in a community that can hold us and allow us to dream. Thus armed, we can read right the signs of the times and opt for a way that does us all good.

Gauchos in Argentina and cowboys in the United States have the same piece of advice: "Don't change horses in midstream." In times of trial you need to be firm in faith, to stay faithful to what matters. A crisis is almost always the result of a self-forgetting, and the way forward comes through recalling our roots.

This is a time to recover values, in the

proper sense of the word: to return to what is authentically worthwhile. The value of life, of nature, of the dignity of the person, of work, of relationship—all these are values key to human life, which cannot be traded away or sacrificed. It amazes me when I hear people talk of "non-negotiable values." All true values, human values, are non-negotiable. Can I say which of the fingers on my hand has more value than the others? If it is of value, it has a value that cannot be negotiated.

Jesus gave us a set of key words with which he summed up the grammar of the Kingdom of God: the Beatitudes. They begin in the hope of the poor for fullness of life, for peace and fraternity, for equity and justice. It is an order of existence in which values are not negotiated but sacrosanct. Reflecting on the Kingdom of God in response to the way we live in the modern world, the Church has developed a series of principles for reflection, together with criteria for judgment that also offer directives for action. It is known as Catholic Social Teaching (CST). While they are drawn from reflection on the Gospel, its principles are accessible to all, seeking to translate and set in motion the Good News in the here and now.

The criteria are truly expressions of love, that is, they seek to set in motion dynamics that allow people to feel loved, especially the poor, who are able to experience their true value. When the Church talks of *the preferential option for the poor,* it means that we need always to keep in mind how any decision we make might impact the poor. But it also means we need to put the poor at the center of our thinking. By means of that preferential option, the Lord gives us a new perspective on value with which to judge events.

Similarly, when the Church speaks of *the common good* it asks us to have regard for the good of society as a whole. It is not enough to adjudicate between different parties and interests, or to think in terms of the greatest happiness of the greatest number, as if the interests of the majority trump all the other interests. The common good is the good we all share in, the good of the people as a whole, as well as the goods we hold in common that should be for all. When we invest in the common good, we amplify what is good for all.

Another principle of social teaching is *the universal destination of goods.* God meant the goods of the earth for all. Private property is a right, but its use and regulation need to keep in mind this key principle. The goods of life—land, lodging, and labor—should be made available to all. This is not altruism, or goodwill; it is what love demands. The early Church fathers made clear that giving to the poor is just giving back to them what is theirs, for God intended the goods of the earth for all, without excluding anyone.

Two other CST principles also matter here: *solidarity* and *subsidiarity*. Solidarity acknowledges our interconnectedness: we are creatures in relationship, with duties toward each other, and all are called to participate in society. That means welcoming the stranger, forgiving debts, giving a home to the disabled, and allowing other people's dreams and hopes for a better life to become our own. But subsidiarity ensures that we do not distort the idea of solidarity, which involves recognizing and respecting the autonomy of others as subjects of their own destiny. The poor are not the objects of our good intentions but the subjects of change. We do not just act for the poor but with them, as Benedict XVI so well explained in the second part of his 2007 encyclical letter *Deus Caritas Est* ("God Is Love").

How do we apply these noble but abstract criteria to the large and small choices we make? This calls for the kind of reflection and prayer known as *discernment of spirits*. Discernment means to think through our decisions and actions, not just by rational calculation but by listening for His Spirit, recognizing in prayer God's motives, invitations, and will. There is a principle worth remembering in these times: ideas are debated, but reality is *discerned*.

This is a difficult thing for those of a more impatient disposition, who believe that to every problem there must be a technical solution, as if it were merely a question of finding the right switch. Many religious people, too, struggle with discernment, especially those who are allergic to uncertainty and want to reduce everything to black and white. And it is quite impossible for ideologues, fundamentalists, and anyone else who is held back by a rigid mindset. But discernment is vital if we want to create a better future.

Coronavirus has accelerated a change of era that was already under way. By "change of era" I mean not just that this is a time of change, but that the categories and assumptions that we used before to navigate our world are no longer effective. Things we never imagined would take place—the environmental collapse, a global pandemic, the return of populisms—we are now living through, and what we once considered normal will increasingly no longer be. It is an illusion to think that we can go back to where we were. Attempts at restoration always take us down a dead-end street.

Faced with this uncertainty, ideology and the rigid mindset have an allure that we must resist. Fundamentalism is a means of assembling thought and behavior as a refuge that supposedly protects a person from a crisis. Fundamentalist mindsets offer to shelter people from destabilizing situations in exchange for a kind of existential quietism. They offer you an attitude and a single, closed way of thinking, as a substitute for the kind of thinking that opens you to truth. Whoever takes refuge in fundamentalism is afraid of setting out on the road to truth. He already "has" the truth, and deploys it as a defense, so that any questioning of it is interpreted as an aggression against his person.

Discernment, on the other hand, allows us to navigate changing contexts and specific situations as we seek the truth. Truth reveals itself to the one who opens herself to it. That is what the ancient Greek word for truth, *aletheia*, means: what reveals itself; what is unveiled. The Hebrew vowel *emet*, on the other hand, connects truth to fidelity, to what is certain, what is firm, what does not deceive or disappoint. So truth has these two elements. When things and people manifest their essence, they give us the certainty of their truth, the trustworthy evidence that invites us to believe in them. Opening ourselves to this kind of certainty calls for humility in our own thinking, to leave space for this gentle encounter with the good, the true, and the beautiful.

I learned this way of thinking from Romano Guardini. It was his style that captivated me, first of all in his book *The Lord*. Guardini showed me the importance of *el pensamiento incompleto*, unfinished thinking. He develops a thought but only takes you so far before he invites you stop to give space to contemplate. He creates room for you to encounter the truth. A fruitful thought should always be unfinished in order to give space to subsequent development. With Guardini I learned not to demand absolute certainties in everything, which is the sign of an anxious spirit. His wisdom has allowed me to confront complex problems that cannot be resolved simply with norms, using instead a kind of thinking that allows you to navigate conflicts without being trapped in them.

The way of thinking that he proposes opens us to the Spirit and to the discernment of spirits. If you don't open up, you can't discern. Hence my allergy to moralisms and other -isms that try to resolve all problems with prescriptions, equations, and rules. Like Guardini, I believe in objective truths and solid principles. I am grateful for the solidity of the Church's tradition, the fruit of centuries of shepherding humanity and of *fides quaerens intellectum*, faith seeking reasoning and understanding. Like John Henry Newman, whom I declared a saint in October 2019, I see the truth lying outside us, always beyond us, but beckoning to us through our consciences. It is like a "kindly light" we reach not normally through reason but "through the imagination, by means of direct impressions, by the testimony of facts and events, by history, by description," as he wrote in *Grammar of Assent*. Newman was convinced, as am I, that in embracing what often appear at first sight to be contradictory truths and trusting in the kindly light to lead us, we will eventually come to see the greater truth that lies beyond us. I like to think that we do not possess the truth so much as the truth possesses us, constantly attracting us by means of beauty and goodness.

This is an approach to truth quite distinct from the epistemology of post-truth, which demands that we choose sides rather than hear evidence. Yet it doesn't mean thinking in set ways that are closed to new possibilities; it contains both an element of assent and an element of continuous searching. That has been the tradition of the Church: her understanding and beliefs have expanded and consolidated over time in openness to the Spirit, according to the principle enunciated in the fifth century by Saint Vincent of Lérins: "They strengthen with the years, develop with time and become deeper with age."[7]

Tradition is not a museum, true religion is not a freezer, and doctrine is not static but grows and develops, like a tree that remains the same yet which gets bigger and bears ever more fruit. There are some who claim that God spoke once and for all time—almost always exclusively in the way and the form that those who make this claim know well. They hear the word "discernment" and worry that it's a fancy way of ignoring the rules or some clever modern ruse to downgrade the truth, when it is quite the opposite. Discernment is as old as the Church. It follows from the promise Jesus made to his disciples that after he was gone the Spirit "will guide you into all the truth" (John 16:13). There is no contradiction between being solidly rooted in the truth and at the same time being open to a greater understanding. The Spirit continues to guide us in our translating the Good News into different contexts, so that the words of Jesus continue to resound in the hearts of men and women in every age. That is why I like to quote Gustav Mahler, that "tradition is not the repository of ashes but the preservation of fire."

The Spirit shows us new things through what the Church calls "signs of the times." Discerning the signs of the times allows us to make sense of change. In interpreting and praying over events or trends in the light of the Gospel, we can detect movements that reflect the values of God's Kingdom or their opposite.

In every age people experience "hunger and thirst for righteousness" (Matthew 5:6), a cry that goes up from the margins of society. If we discern in such a yearning a movement of God's Spirit, it allows us to open up to that movement in thought and action, and so create a new future according to the spirit of the Beatitudes.

For example, one sad sign of our times is

the exclusion and isolation of the elderly. A significant number of all Covid-19 deaths have been in elderly care homes. Those who died were vulnerable not just because of their age but because of the conditions in many of those homes: underfunded, neglected, dependent on a high turnover of poorly paid workers. I often went to such homes in Buenos Aires, where the caregivers do an amazing job in spite of so many obstacles. I remember once them telling me that many of the residents hadn't been seen by their relatives in at least six months. The abandonment of the elderly is an enormous injustice.

Scripture tells us that the elderly are our roots, our source, our sustenance. The prophet Joel hears God's promise to pour out His Spirit to renew His people: "Your sons and your daughters shall prophesy, your old men shall dream dreams, and your young men shall see visions" (Joel 2:28). The future will be born from the conjunction of the young and the old. As Francisco Luis Bernárdez, an Argentine poet, puts it: "At the end of it all I've understood / that what on the tree flowers / lives from what is buried."[8] A tree separated from its roots does not flower or fruit, but dries up. So here we have two ills with the same cause: the abandonment of the elderly deprived of the visions of the young, and the impoverishment of the young deprived of the dreams of the old; and a society that dries up, becomes fruitless, and sterile.

In the light of the Gospel and our Catholic social principles—solidarity, subsidiarity, option for the poor, universal destination of goods—it is impossible not to feel the need to put everything into overcoming that gap so that the generations encounter each other. How do we welcome the elderly back into families, restore their contact with the young? How do we give young people the roots so they can prophesy, that is, open spaces for themselves to grow in? Discernment comes in at this point: What does this mean for me and my family? What does this mean for our public policies? We might wonder the same about unemployed young people deprived of the chance to study, often drawn to the sad world of drugs.

We may feel a prompting of the Spirit to find out who are the lonely elderly nearby, and how with others I could offer them friendship. Or I might want to ensure that care homes are as much like families as possible, well funded and embedded in community. At a deeper level, we may wonder how we ended up in this situation, under pressure from jobs and families who convince people they cannot have the elderly living with them.

We see the reality, we discern, and we discover there a sign from God. We do not claim to have the answers, but applying the Gospel's criteria and sensing the prompting of the Spirit, discernment allows us to hear the Lord's invitation and to follow it. Our life becomes, as a result, richer and more prophetic, allowing us to respond with the depth that only the Holy Spirit can give us.

The change of era, accelerated by coronavirus, is a propitious moment for reading the signs of the times. A gap has opened up between the realities and challenges we face and the recipes and solutions available to us. That gap becomes a space in which to reflect, question, and dialogue.

Consider, for example, the distance between our need to protect and regenerate Mother Earth and an economic model that regards growth at any cost as its prime objective.

Of course, some regions—very underdeveloped areas, or countries recovering from war—need their economies to grow rapidly to meet their people's basic needs. But in the wealthier parts of the world, the fixation with constant economic growth has become destabilizing, producing vast inequalities and putting the natural world out of balance. Unlimited expansion of productivity and consumption assumes human dominance over creation, but the environmental disaster it has brought about has shattered the assumptions of that thinking. We are part of creation; we do not own it: to some extent, it owns us; we cannot live apart from it. This crisis or breach is a sign of our time.

The disruption of Covid has turned the tables, inviting us to stop, alter our routines and priorities, and to ask: What if the economic, the social, and the ecological challenges we face are really different faces of the same crisis? What if they have a common solution? Could it be that replacing the objective of growth with that of new ways of relating will allow for a different kind of economy, one that meets the needs of all within the means of our planet?

The discernment step allows us to ask: What is the Spirit telling us? What is the grace on offer here, if we can only embrace it; and what are the obstacles and temptations? What humanizes, what dehumanizes? Where is the good news hidden within the somber news, and where is the bad spirit dressed as an angel of light? These are questions for those who humbly search and listen, who are willing not just to grasp at answers but to reflect and pray.

Be careful of those who claim now to see the future with a kind of clarity and security. In crises "false Messiahs" always appear who ignore the freedom of the people to build their own future, and who close themselves to the action of God entering into the life and history of His people. God acts in the simplicity of open hearts, in the patience of those who pause until they can see clearly.

Discerning what is and what is not of God, we begin to see where and how to act. When we find where God's mercy is waiting to overflow, we can open the gates, and work with all people of goodwill to bring about the necessary changes.

How do we distinguish the spirits? They speak different languages; they use different ways to reach our hearts. The voice of God never imposes but proposes, whereas the enemy is strident, insistent, and even monotonous. The voice of God might correct us, but gently, always encouraging, consoling, giving us hope. The bad spirit on the other hand offers us dazzling illusions and tempting sensations, but they are fleeting. It exploits our fears and suspicions, and seduces us with wealth and prestige. If we ignore it, it responds with contempt and accusation, telling us: You're worthless.

The voice of the enemy distracts us from the present by getting us to focus on fears of the future or the sadness of the past. The voice of God, on the other hand, speaks to the present, helping us to move ahead in the here and now. What comes from God asks: "What is good for me, what is good for us?"

The voice of God opens your horizons, whereas the enemy pins you against a wall. Where the good spirit gives you hope, the bad spirit sows suspicion, anxiety, and finger-pointing. The good spirit appeals to my desire to do good, to help and serve, and gives me strength to go forward on the right path. The bad spirit, conversely, closes me in on myself, and makes me rigid and intolerant. It is the spirit of fear and grievance. It makes me sad, fearful, and irritable. Rather than freeing me, it enslaves me. Rather than opening me up to the present and the future, it encloses me in fear and resignation.

Learning to distinguish these two kinds of "voice" allows us to choose the right path forward, which is not always the most obvious, and to avoid making decisions while trapped in past hurts or in fears of the future that risk immobilizing us.

A sign is something that stands out and strikes us. A sign of hope in this crisis is the leading role of women.

Women have been at the same time among the most affected and the most resilient in this crisis. Affected, because they are more likely to be on the front line of the pandemic—about 70 percent of all those working in health care worldwide are women—but also because they are harder hit economically while working in the informal or unpaid sector.

The countries with women as presidents or prime ministers have on the whole reacted better and more quickly than others, making decisions swiftly and communicating them with empathy.

What does this sign invite us to think about? What might the Spirit be saying to us?

I think of the strength of the women in the Gospel following the death of Jesus. They were not paralyzed by the tragedy, nor did they flee. For love of the Master, they went to the tomb to anoint Him. Like so many women in this pandemic, they were able to hold it together, to get around obstacles in their path and keep hope alive in their families and in the community. Because they did so, they were the first to receive the astonishing news: "He is not here; for he has been raised" (Matthew 28:6). The Lord first announced the New Life to women because they were present, attentive, open to new possibilities.

Could it be that in this crisis the perspective women bring is what the world needs at this time to face the coming challenges?

Could the Spirit be prompting us to recognize, value, and integrate the fresh thinking that some women are bringing to this moment?

I am thinking in particular of women economists whose fresh thinking is especially relevant for this crisis. Their call for an overhaul of the models we use to manage economies is attracting attention. Theirs is a perspective born of their practical experience of the "real" economy, which they say has opened their eyes to the inadequacy of standard textbook economics. It was often their unpaid or informal work, their experience of maternity or running households in addition to high-level academic work, that made them aware of the flaws in the dominant economic models of at least the last seventy years.

I don't mean to put them in the same basket just because they are all women. They are each different from each other, and no doubt disagree about many things. Yet it is striking how these influential economists have put the focus on areas long sidelined by mainstream thinking, such as care for creation and for the poor, the value of nonmonetized relationships and the public sector, as well as the contribution of civil society to generating wealth. I see them advocating a more "maternal" economy, one that isn't focused solely on growth and profit but asks how economies can be geared to helping people to participate in society and thrive. They advocate an economy that sustains, protects, and regenerates, not just regulates and arbitrates. Such ideas, long dismissed as idealistic or unrealistic, now seem prescient and relevant.[9]

Mariana Mazzucato's book *The Value of Everything* provoked a lot of reflection in me. I was struck by the way that business successes lauded in our economic thinking as the result of individuals' efforts or genius are in reality the fruit of massive public investment in research and education. Yet the shareholders collect vast profits, and the state is regarded as placing a burden on the market. Or I think of Kate Raworth, an economist at Oxford University, who talks of "doughnut economics": how to create a distributive, regenerative economy that moves people out of the "hole" of destitution but avoids the "ceiling" of environmental damage. Like Mazzucato, she challenges our culture's unthinking obsession with growth in gross domestic product (GDP) as the single overriding goal of economists and policymakers. I could mention others, but these two are known to me especially because of their contributions to the Vatican's thinking about a post-Covid future.

My concern is not to assess their theories—I am not qualified—but to assess the *ethos* of this thinking. I see ideas formed from their experience in the periphery, reflecting a concern about the grotesque inequality of billions facing extreme deprivation while the richest one percent own half of the world's financial wealth. I see an attentiveness to human vulnerability; a desire to protect the natural world by seeing pollution as a cost that must be offset against the balance sheet. I see a concern for economies that allow all who can to access work, and that place a higher value on work that generates not just wealth for shareholders but also value for society. I see thinking that is not ideological, which moves beyond the polarization of free market capitalism and state socialism, and which has at its heart a concern that all of humanity have access to land, lodging, and labor. All of these speak to priorities of the Gospel and the principles of the Church's social doctrine. It is reasonable, then, to see this "rethinking" by women economists as a sign of our time that we should pay attention to.

The attitude of discernment presumes also an awareness of temptations that distract us from the Spirit's message, temptations that can take us down blind alleys. The temptations can be detected by their rigidity and uniformity. Where the Spirit is present, there is always a movement *versus in unum*, toward unity, but never toward uniformity. The Spirit always preserves the legitimate plurality of different groups and points of view, reconciling them in their diversity. Thus, if a group or person were to insist that their way is the only way of "reading" a sign, that would be a warning light.

For example, a temptation of rigid thinking is to reduce people to their functions. A functionalist error might be to believe that integrating the perspective of women *necessarily* means appointing more women to executive roles, because only when women have more "power" will their perspectives gain ground. But if the contribution of women also *challenges* assumptions of power, it does not necessarily follow that a woman leader will change an institution's culture. This goes beyond any specific positions of responsibility they may hold. I take for granted, of course, that qualified women should have equal access to leadership, equivalent salaries, and other opportunities; that right has been one of the great social gains of modern times. But it may be worth asking if there are other ways of allowing women's perspectives to challenge existing assumptions.

This is something that has concerned me in Rome: how better to integrate the presence and sensibility of women into the Vatican's decision-making processes. The challenge for me has been to create spaces where women can lead, but in ways that allow them to shape the culture, ensuring they are valued, respected, and recognized. The women I have appointed are there because of their skills and experience, but also to influence the vision and mindset of the Church's bureaucracy. In many cases I have invited women to be consultants to Vatican bodies, so that they can influence the Vatican while preserving their independence from it. Changing institutional culture is an organic process which calls for integrating, without clericalizing, the viewpoints of women.[10]

For some time there have been a number of

women in important Vatican roles. For example in the Dicastery for Laity, Family and Life, the two subsecretaries—section heads, who carry forward the department business—are women. The director of the Vatican Museums is also a woman. But the highest-ranking post is in the Secretariat of State, where the undersecretary for relations with states is a woman who has responsibility for the Church's relations with multilateral organizations such as the United Nations and the Council of Europe.[11]

I've named other women to significant posts, but because those appointments were made one at a time over a period of years they haven't attracted much attention. But when, in 2020, I named a group of six women to the Council for the Economy, the nomination was news. In a body responsible for overseeing the financial management and policies of the Vatican made up of seven cardinals and seven laypeople, it is striking that six of the latter are women.

I chose these particular women because of their qualifications but also because I believe women in general are much better administrators than men. They understand processes better, how to take projects forward. So in these cases they not only had the expertise and professional background we needed—which plenty of men also had—but they also brought their personal experience in organizing day-to-day life in different ways, as mothers and "housewives," and members of discussion groups.

To describe women as "housewives" is often considered demeaning, and sometimes it is used as such. But in Spanish, *ama de casa* ("the mistress of the house") carries the meaning of the Greek *oikos* and *nomos*, from where we get the word "economics": the art of household management. Managing households is no small feat; you have to do many different things at once, reconciling different interests, being flexible, and having a kind of canniness. Housewives have to speak three languages at the same time: that of the mind, that of the heart, and that of the hands.

In my pastoral experience on different Church bodies, some of the sharpest advice came from women who were able to see from different angles, and who were above all *practical,* with a realistic understanding of how things work and people's limitations and potential. Before I was Pope, as archbishop in Buenos Aires I had women as financial director, chancellor, and head of the diocesan archive. I found that the advice of women in pastoral and administrative councils was more valuable than that of many men.

I want to make clear that an expanded role for women in Church leadership doesn't depend on the Vatican and is not limited to specific roles. Perhaps because of clericalism, which is a corruption of the priesthood, many people wrongly believe that Church leadership is exclusively male. But if you go to any diocese in the world you'll see women running departments, schools, hospitals, and many other organizations and programs; in some areas, you'll find many more women than men as leaders. In Amazonia, women—both laypeople and religious sisters— run whole Church communities. To say they aren't truly leaders because they aren't priests is clericalist and disrespectful.

To dream of a different future we need to choose fraternity over individualism as our organizing principle. Fraternity, the sense of belonging to each other and to the whole of humanity, is the capacity to come together and work together against a shared horizon of possibility. In the Jesuit tradition we call this *unión de ánimos*, union of hearts and minds. It's a unity that allows people to serve as a body despite differences of viewpoint, physical separation, and human ego. Such a union preserves and respects plurality, inviting all to contribute from their distinctiveness, as a community of brothers and sisters concerned for each other.

We sorely need this kind of unity. The pandemic has exposed the paradox that while we are more interconnected, we are also more divided. Feverish consumerism breaks the bonds of belonging. It causes us to focus on our self-preservation and makes us anxious. Our fears are exacerbated and exploited by a certain kind of populist politics that seeks power over society. It is hard to build a culture of encounter, in which we meet as people with a shared dignity, within a throwaway culture which regards the elderly, the unemployed, the disabled, and the unborn as surplus to our well-being. This is why I recently wrote a letter to all people of goodwill, inspired by Saint Francis of Assisi, in the hope of rekindling a desire for fraternity.[12]

Before discussing how we can overcome some of the breaches and divisions in our society to build peace and the common good, we need to consider the "isolated conscience," which acts as a major obstacle to the union of hearts and minds. Perhaps if I talk about how it operates in the Church, people might find it applicable to other institutions and society at large.

No matter which realm we're examining, it's important to understand the effect of a bad-spirit temptation to withdraw spiritually from the body to which I belong, closing us in on our own interests and viewpoints by means of suspicion and supposition. And how this temptation turns us, ultimately, into beleaguered, complaining selves who disdain others, believing that we alone know the truth.[13]

In the history of the Church there have always existed groups that have ended up in heresy because of this temptation to a pride that made them feel superior to the Body of Christ. In our own time, since the Second Vatican Council (1962–65), we have had revolutionary ideologies followed by restorationist ones. In every case, what marks them out is rigidity. Rigidity is the sign of the bad spirit concealing something. What is hidden might not be revealed for a long time, until some scandal erupts. We've seen more than a few Church groups in recent years—movements almost always marked by their rigidity and authoritarianism—end up this way. Leaders and other members presented themselves as restorers of doctrine and of the Church, but what we later learn of their lives tells us the opposite. Behind every group seeking to impose its ideology on the Church, you find the same rigidity. Sooner or later there'll be some shocking revelation involving sex, money, or mind control.

What is hidden is an attempt to cling to something petty I fear to lose, something that feeds my ego: power, influence, freedom, security, status, money, property, or some combination of these. My fear of losing what Saint Ignatius calls "this acquired fortune" leads me to cling more tightly to it, such that when I am asked to step out and become part of something bigger, the spirit of suspicion and supposition supplies reasons to hold back, concealing my attachments while justifying them through the faults of others. Little by little, as I embrace these "reasons" that justify my self-withholding, my heart hardens and my commitment to these reasons increases, turning them eventually into an ideology.[14]

Thus, among Catholics of an isolated conscience, there is never a shortage of reasons for criticizing the Church, the bishops, or the Pope: either we are behind the times, or we have surrendered to modernity; we are not what we should be or supposedly once were. In this way, they justify withholding and separating themselves from the forward march of the People of God. Rather than throwing themselves into the great task of evangelizing our world in communion with the Body, they remain huddled in "their" group of purists, guardians of the truth. To the self beleaguered by the isolated conscience there is never a shortage of reasons for staying on the balcony while real life passes below.

Thus are sown the seeds of division. A charitable openness to the other is replaced by a clinging to the supposed superiority of one's own ideas. Unity is undermined by a battle between different parties who struggle to impose the hegemony of their ideas. Under the banner of restoration or reform, people give long speeches and write endless articles offering doctrinal clarifications or manifestos that reflect little more than the obsessions of small groups. Meanwhile, the people called together by God moves forward in the footsteps of Jesus, not blind to the faults of the Church but happy to be part of His Body, confessing their sins and imploring mercy. The People of God recognizes its faults and sins, and is able to ask forgiveness because it knows itself to be a people that has been shown mercy.

These faults and shortcomings are well-known. Some people have painful experiences that make their distrust of the Church understandable. My concern here is with a spiritual condition that shows itself in the arrogance of believing that the Church needs to be saved from itself, or that treats the Church as if it were a corporation whose shareholders can demand a change of management. This is a version of spiritual worldliness. Those who declare there is too much "confusion" in the Church, and that only this or that group of purists or traditionalists can be trusted, sow division in the Body. This, too, is spiritual worldliness. The same is true of those who claim that until the Church ordains women as proof of its commitment to gender equality, the local parish or bishop cannot count on their involvement. Outwardly, the reasons appear coherent and principled, but they disguise the spirit of the isolated conscience, which refuses to act as a disciple of Christ within His Church.

Jesus did not found the Church as a citadel of purity nor as a constant parade of heroes and saints—although thank God we do not lack these. It is something much more dynamic: a school of conversion, a place of spiritual combat and discernment, where grace abounds along with sin and temptation. Like its members, the Church can be an instrument of God's mercy because it needs that mercy. Just as none of us should reject other people because of their sins and failures but help them be what they are meant to be, Christ's followers should love and listen to the Church, build her up, take responsibility for her, including her sins and failures. At those moments when the Church shows herself to be weak and sinful, let us help her get up again; let us not condemn or disdain her, but care for her like our own mother.

The isolated conscience finds it hard to treat others with mercy because it rejects such mercy, at least in practice. The biblical example par excellence of the beleaguered self is the prophet Jonah. God sends Jonah to Nineveh to invite the people there to repent but Jonah is having none of it, and flees to Tarshish. In reality what Jonah flees is God's mercy for Nineveh, which doesn't fit with his plans and mindset. For Jonah, God came once, handed down a law, and "I'll take care of the rest," Jonah says to himself. In his mind he was saved and the Ninevites were not; he had the truth and they did not; he was in charge and God was not. He had erected a fence around his soul with the barbed wire of his certainties, dividing the world into good and bad, and closing off the door to God's action. How the heart of the beleaguered self hardens when it comes into contact with God's mercy!

Today, sadly, so many people act like Jonah before he softened. From the closed world of their beleaguered selves they complain and disdain; and feeling their identities threatened, get involved in battles—online and in person—in order to feel more secure.

It's remarkable how quickly the isolated conscience deteriorates, spiritually and psychologically. Having separated them from the body of the People of God, the devil continues to feed such people fallacies and half-truths that close them off ever more in their Tarshishes of self-righteousness. (The devil does not only tempt with lies. Often a half-truth, or a truth uprooted from its spiritual foundation, works better because it makes it harder for people to communicate with each other.) These people end up trading doctrine for ideology, and their suspicions and suppositions lead them ultimately into conspiracy theories, viewing everything through a distorted lens. Thus, abandoned to itself, the isolated conscience can end up believing many strange fantasies without need of proof.

For example, at the Synod on Amazonia in Rome in October 2019 some groups in the

Church and their media reported the presence of indigenous people through a continuously distorted lens. What was beautiful in that synod—the deep respect for indigenous culture and the presence of the native people in the prayer services—was twisted by hysterical accusations of paganism and syncretism. Although we were barely aware of it inside the synod hall, there was no shortage of disturbances outside. The indignation of the isolated conscience begins in unreality, passes through Manichaean fantasies that divide the world into good and bad (with themselves always on the good side), and ends in different kinds of violence: verbal, physical, and so on.

There is no vaccination against the isolated conscience of the beleaguered self but there is an antidote. It is freely available, and costs nothing but our pride. "Self-accusation" is a simple notion set down by a sixth-century desert monk, Dorotheus of Gaza, drawing on the wisdom of the desert fathers who showed how God never leaves us alone in temptations. In accusing ourselves, we "lower" ourselves, making room for the action of God to unite us. Just as the isolated conscience comes about by accusing others, so, too, unity is the fruit of accusing ourselves. Rather than justifying ourselves—the spirit of self-sufficiency and arrogance—self-accusation expresses what Jesus in the Beatitudes calls poverty of spirit. It's the contrast he draws between the tax collector and the Pharisee in Luke 18:9–14: the tax collector prays, "God, be merciful to me, a sinner!" while the other—who thanks God for not being like others—isn't able to pray.

This act of "lowering myself" imitates the coming-down and coming-close of the Word of God, the *synkatabasis*. It is the humility of confessing our faults, not to punish ourselves—which would make the same mistake of putting ourselves in charge—but to acknowledge our dependence on God and our need of His grace. Rather than accusing others for their failures and limitations, I find some fault or attitude in myself. And I then turn to my Creator and my God and ask Him for the grace I need to move forward, confident that He loves me and cares for me. Rather than close myself off to God, I open the door for Him to act in and through me, because God never imposes on our freedom; He must be invited in. And I find, when this happens, that rather than find fault in my brother or sister, I see in him or her one who is also struggling and in need of help, and I offer myself in service to them.

Accusing myself, confident of God's mercy, reveals the bad spirit, which loses its foothold. Often what divides us comes not from holding different views but from the bad spirit hidden behind those views, which remains hidden by the contagious cycle of accusation and counteraccusation. Just as what separates me from my brother and sister is my (and their) spirit of self-sufficiency and superiority, so what unites us is our shared insufficiency, our mutual dependence on God and on each other. We are no longer rivals, but members of the same family. We might argue and disagree, but we are no longer caught in a vicious spiral of mutual antagonism. We do not think the same, but we are part of the same Body moving together.

Just as Jonah is the icon of the isolated conscience, the publican Zacchaeus (Luke 19:1–10) is the great example of one who renounces his isolation. Zacchaeus was a tax collector who lived off his people. But when Jesus came to his town Zacchaeus climbed up a tree to catch sight of him; there was a desire in him to be free from the cold loneliness to which his isolated conscience had led him. Jesus calls the tax collector down from his self-sufficiency to join the people, and Zacchaeus promises to put his wealth at the service of others. He accepts mercy and is changed by mercy. Now he is free to build a new future, alongside others, from below, in the patient struggle that burns away all arrogance.

The way of accusation of others ignores God; self-accusation opens us to Him. Before God, none of us is innocent, but all of us are forgiven when we recognize and repent our sins and feel shame for our faults. In this way we are freed from seeing our opponents as our enemies. Self-accusation is the antibody to the virus of the isolated conscience, and humility before God the key that unlocks fraternity and social peace.

Don't let the wrong you believe another has done to you trigger your descent into the isolated conscience. As Dorotheus puts it, "Suspicions and suppositions are full of malice and never leave the soul in peace."[15]

As the public arena has become increasingly dominated by the beleaguered self—anxious, controlling, quick to take offense, self-justifying—our society risks becoming ever more divided and fragmented. The Church is not immune to the contagion. How do we act in contexts of tribal division when our politics, our society, our media seem at times to be one long shouting match, in which opponents seek to "cancel" each other in a game of power? The growing verbal violence reflects a fragility of selfhood, a loss of roots, in which security is found in discrediting others through narratives that let us feel righteous and give us reasons for silencing others. The absence of sincere dialogue in our public culture makes it ever harder to generate a shared horizon toward which we can all move forward together.

As the paralysis of polarization sets in, public life is reduced to a squabble between factions seeking supremacy. In my address to the U.S. Congress in 2015, I highlighted the temptation of a simplistic reductionism that sees only good or evil, or the righteous and sinners—the Jonah syndrome I mentioned earlier. I said in Congress: "The contemporary world, with its open wounds which affect so many of our brothers and sisters, demands that we confront every form of polarization which would divide it into these two camps. We know that in the attempt to be freed of the enemy without, we can be tempted to feed the enemy within."[16]

I spoke of the "enemy within" because polarization also has a spiritual root. Polarization is amplified and exacerbated by some media and some politicians, but it is born in the heart. When we are in a polarized environment, we must be aware of the bad spirit which enters into division and creates a downward spiral of accusation and counteraccusation. An ancient term for the devil is the Great Accuser. Here, in verbal violence, in defamation, and in superfluous cruelty, we find his cave. It's best not to enter. You don't argue or dialogue with the Accuser, because that is to adopt his logic, in which spirits are disguised as reasons. You need to resist him with other means, throwing him out, as Jesus did. Like coronavirus, if the virus of polarization cannot transfer from host to host, it gradually disappears.

Instead of letting ourselves become trapped within the labyrinth of accusation and counteraccusation, which conceals the bad spirit in a tissue of false reasons and justifications, we need to allow the bad spirit to reveal itself. This is what Jesus teaches us from the Cross. In gentleness and powerlessness, he forced the devil to show himself: the Accuser confuses silence with weakness, and redoubles his attack, revealing his fury, and thereby who he is.

Our main task, however, is not to disengage from polarization but to engage with conflict and disagreement in ways that prevent us from descending into polarization. This means resolving division by allowing for new thinking that can transcend that division. In this way, divisions do not generate sterile polarizations but bear valuable new fruit. This is a vital task for our time of crisis. Faced with huge challenges that must be tackled on many fronts at the same time, we need to practice the art of civic dialogue that synthesizes different views on a higher plane.

This kind of politics is more than campaigning and debating, when the objective is to persuade and defeat. It is more like an act of charity, in which we search for solutions together for the benefit of all. For this mission, we need the humility to dispense with what we come to see as wrong, and the courage to take on board points of view other than our own that contain elements of truth.

The task of "holding" disagreement and allowing it to become a link in a new process is a valuable mission for all of us. When Jesus said: "Blessed are the peacemakers" (Matthew 5:9), this is surely the mission He meant.

Guardini gave me a startling insight to deal with conflicts, analyzing their complexity while avoiding any simplifying reductionism: there exist differences in tension, pulling apart, but all coexist within a larger unity.

Understanding how apparent contradictions could be resolved metaphysically, through discernment, was the topic of my thesis on Guardini, which I went to Germany to research. I worked on it for some years but never finished writing it up. But the thesis has helped me a lot, especially in managing tensions and conflicts. (Twenty years later, in 2012, after I turned seventy-five, when I thought Pope Benedict might accept my resignation as Archbishop of Buenos Aires, it occurred to me for a time that I might, after all, finish the thesis. But in March 2013 I was transferred to another diocese. In the end I gave what I had written to a priest who was studying Guardini.)[17]

One of the effects of conflict is to see as

contradictions what are in fact contrapositions, as I like to call them. A contraposition involves two poles in tension, pulling away from each other: horizon/limit, local/global, whole/part, and so on. These are contrapositions because they are opposites that nonetheless interact in a fruitful, creative tension. As Guardini taught me, creation is full of these living polarities, or *Gegensätze*; they are what make us alive and dynamic. Contradictions (*Widersprüche*) on the other hand demand that we choose, between right and wrong. (Good and evil can never be a contraposition, because evil is not the counterpart of good but its negation.)

To see contrapositions as contradictions is the result of mediocre thinking that takes us away from reality. The bad spirit—the spirit of conflict, which undermines dialogue and fraternity— turns contrapositions into contradictions, demanding we choose, and reducing reality to simple binaries. This is what ideologies and unscrupulous politicians do. So when we run up against a contradiction that does not allow us to advance to a real solution, we know we are faced with a reductive, partial mental scheme that we must try to move beyond.

But the bad spirit can also deny the tension between two poles in a contraposition, opting instead for a kind of static coexistence. This is the danger of relativism or false irenicism, an attitude of "peace at any price" in which the goal is to avoid conflict altogether. In this case, there can be no solution, because the tension has been denied, and abandoned. This is also a refusal to accept reality.

So we have two temptations: on the one hand, to wrap ourselves in the banner of one side or the other, exacerbating the conflict; on the other, to avoid engaging in conflict altogether, denying the tension involved and washing our hands of it.

The task of the reconciler is instead to "endure" the conflict, facing it head-on, and by discerning see beyond the surface reasons for disagreement, opening those involved to the possibility of a new synthesis, one that does not destroy either pole, but preserves what is good and valid in both in a new perspective.

This breakthrough comes about as a gift in dialogue, when people trust each other and humbly seek the good together, and are willing to learn from each other in a mutual exchange of gifts. At such moments, the solution to an intractable problem comes in ways that are unexpected and unforeseen, the result of a new and greater creativity released, as it were, from the outside. This is what I mean by "overflow" because it breaks the banks that confined our thinking, and causes to pour forth, as if from an overflowing fountain, the answers that formerly the contraposition didn't let us see. We recognize this process as a gift from God because it is the same action of the Spirit described in Scripture and evident in history.

"Overflow" is one possible translation of the Greek *perisseuo*, which is the word used by the psalmist whose cup overflows with God's grace in Psalm 23. *Perisseuo* was what Jesus promises (Luke 6:38) will be poured into our laps when we forgive. It is the noun deployed in John's Gospel (John 10:10) to describe the life that Jesus came to bring, and the adjective Saint Paul uses (2 Corinthians 1:5) to describe God's generosity. It is the very heart of God that overflows in those famous passages of the father rushing out to hug his prodigal son, the wedding host who gathers guests from the roads and the fields for his banquet, the net-breaking catch of fish at dawn after a night of fruitless trawling, or Jesus washing the feet of his disciples on the night before he died.

Such overflows of love happen, above all, at the crossroads of life, at moments of openness, fragility, and humility, when the ocean of His love bursts the dams of our self-sufficiency, and so allows for a new imagination of the possible.

My concern as Pope has been to encourage such overflows within the Church by reinvigorating the ancient practice of synodality. I have wanted to develop this ancient process not just for the sake of the Church but as a service to a humanity that is so often locked in paralyzed disagreements.

The term comes from the Greek *syn-odos*, "walking together," and this is its goal: not so much to forge agreement as to recognize, honor, and reconcile differences on a higher plane where the best of each can be retained. In the dynamic of a synod, differences are expressed and polished until you reach, if not consensus, a harmony that holds on to the sharp notes of its differences. This is what happens in music: with seven different musical notes with their sharps and flats a harmony is created that allows for the better articulation of the singularities of each note. Therein lies its beauty: the harmony that results can be complex, rich, and unexpected. In the Church the one who brings about that harmony is the Holy Spirit.

I like to see the beginning of ecclesial synodality in the early Church when the apostles gathered to wrestle with a question that divided them: Should non-Jewish people be bound by Jewish laws and customs such as circumcision when they become Christian? After discussion and prayer and some bitter disagreement, they pondered the way that God had worked signs and wonders among them through the Gentiles, for God is recognized in the experience of real life. They declared that "it has seemed good to

110

the Holy Spirit and to us" (Acts 15:28) not to impose on non-Jewish Christians the regulations of Jewish law.

It was a new opening that changed the course of history. God had made a covenant of salvation with a single people, the Jewish people, which Christ recovered and offered to all of humanity, irrespective of race, nation, or language. This is why Christianity has never been confined to a particular culture but has been enriched by the cultures of the peoples where it has taken root. Each of these peoples experiences the gift of God according to its own culture, and in each of them the Church expresses its genuine Catholicity, the beauty of its many different faces.

The synod experience allows us to walk together not just in spite of our differences, but seeking the truth and taking on the richness of the polar tensions at stake. Many breakthroughs have happened in councils and assemblies throughout the Church's history. But what matters most is that harmony that enables us to move forward together on the same path, even with all our shades of difference.

This synodal approach is something our world now needs badly. Rather than seeking confrontation, declaring war, with each side hoping to defeat the other, we need processes that allow differences to be expressed, heard, and left to mature in such a way that we can walk together without needing to destroy anyone. This is hard work; it needs patience and commitment—above all to each other. Lasting peace is about creating and maintaining processes of mutual listening. We build a people not with the weapons of war but in the productive tension of walking together.

In this task, mediators matter. Making agreements that prevent rupture and allow all sides to keep walking together is a vital role of law and politics. Mediation is a science, but also an exercise in human wisdom. In law and politics the mediator plays a role analogous, in some ways, to that of the Holy Spirit in the synod, holding together differences until new horizons open up.

At its best, this is what happens, for example, in the European Union: achieving reconciliation in difference. The EU has been through a difficult period. But to watch its members reach agreement on a coronavirus bailout package—all those different agendas and views, the furious trading and negotiation—was an example of this attempt to harmonize differences within an overall effort to seek unity. That is what I mean when I compare this with synodality, and why perhaps our experience within the Church can help our world at large. Let's look at what happens, and perhaps learn some lessons.

There have been three synods during my time as Pope: on the family, on young people, and on Amazonia. At each, more than two hundred bishops and cardinals and laypeople gathered from across the world to carry out a discernment over a period usually of three weeks, at the end of which the bishops voted on the concluding document. This process, instituted by Saint Paul VI, has grown and developed, raising along the way new questions to answer. That is why I would like to see, in the future, a synod on the topic of synodality. The changes I have introduced so far mean that the synods held every two or three years here in Rome are freer and more dynamic, giving more time for honest discussion and listening.[18]

Synodality starts with hearing from the whole People of God. A Church that teaches must be firstly a Church that listens. The Master was a good master because he knew how to be a good disciple (Philippians 2:6–11). Consulting all members of the Church is vital because, as the Second Vatican Council reminded us, the faithful as a whole are anointed by the Holy Spirit and "cannot err in matters of belief."[19]

So each of the Synods held in Rome started from wide-ranging discussions and consultations organized in local Churches who gathered up themes and concerns articulated in the "preparatory document" to be discussed. Many different voices and perspectives are included in the assembly itself: laypeople, invited experts, and delegates from other (non-Catholic) Churches, who make vital contributions to the discernment. In this way, we obey a principle that was dear to the Church of the first millennium: *Quod omnes tangit ab omnibus tractari debet* (What affects all should be discussed by all).[20]

That's why it delights me to see how the Church in different countries is embarking on processes that put the synod method into practice. In Australia, for example, they have a process going on over several years that involves hundreds of thousands of people, asking how they as a Church can be more inclusive, merciful, and prayerful, and more open to conversion, renewal, and mission.

In speaking of synodality, it's important not to confuse Catholic doctrine and tradition with the Church's norms and practices. What is under discussion at synodal gatherings are not traditional truths of Christian doctrine. The Synod is concerned mainly with how teaching can be lived and applied in the changing contexts of our time. The three Synods—on the Family (2014 and 2015), on Young People (2018), and on Amazonia (2019)—have played a vital role in opening up new ways of caring for people and places facing particular challenges.

What characterizes a synodal path is the role of the Holy Spirit. We listen, we discuss in groups, but above all we pay attention to what the Spirit has to say to us. That is why I ask everyone to speak frankly and to listen carefully to others because, there, too, the Spirit is speaking. Open to changes and new possibilities, the Synod is for everyone an experience of conversion. Hence one of the changes in the process: periods of silence between speeches to allow those in attendance to be better aware of the motions of the Spirit.

Synods produce intense discussion, which is good: they involve different reactions and responses to those who think differently or have particular positions. We do not all react in the same way. We have also seen in many cases how, faced with disagreement, different groups attempting to interfere in the synodal process try to impose their ideas, either by applying pressure inside the Synod, or outside it, by distorting and discrediting the views of those who do not think as they do.

This, too, is a good sign, because wherever the Spirit of God is present, so, too, are temptations to silence it or distract from it. (If the Spirit weren't present, those forces wouldn't bother.) We saw the bad spirit in some of the "noise" outside the synod hall, as well as within it: in the fear, the panic, the claims that the Synod is a conspiracy to undermine Church doctrine, that the Church is closed to new ways of thinking, and so on. These are signs of the isolated conscience we were speaking of earlier, and of the frustration of the bad spirit, which, when it fails to seduce, hurls furious accusations (but never, of course, *self*-accusations).

In the synod hall there also exists the temptation to resist what a synodal process involves: arrogating the monopoly of the interpretation of truth, and trying to impose one's ideas on the whole Body through pressure or by discrediting those who feel differently. Some participants were quick to take up hard-line positions that betrayed an obsession with the purity of doctrine, as if it were under threat and they were its guardians. Others insisted on progressive criteria that are not in keeping with the Gospel and Tradition. This is one of the gifts of the Spirit in the synod process: to unmask agendas and hidden ideologies. That is why we cannot speak of synodality unless we accept and live the presence of the Holy Spirit.

The Gospel must be read and interpreted in the light of the history of salvation and Tradition. Other tools can help to grow our understanding by highlighting, identifying, and valuing hitherto unexplored riches from this source of Living Water.

Another temptation that so often confuses people is treating the Synod as a kind of parliament underpinned by a "political battle" in which in order to govern one side must defeat the other. Some people tried to drum up support for their positions as politicians might: by sounding warnings through the media, or appealing to opinion polls. This goes against the spirit of the synod as a protected space of community discernment.

The media have a key role to play in opening the Synod to the People of God, and the wider world, communicating and helping people see the issues and challenges the Church is facing. But in some cases journalists run the risk of confusing contrapositions with polarizations, reducing the synod dynamic to simplistic yes-no binaries as if the Synod were a dramatic showdown between opposing forces. That is not how it feels inside the synod hall. However, sometimes the media narrative ends up undermining the capacity for discernment.

We saw this in the Synod on the Family, where the aim was to move beyond some of the "casuistic" thinking that prevents the Church from dealing with difficult cases with the nuanced approach of its own healthy Tradition. Jesus condemns the casuistry of the doctors of the law, for example, in chapter 23 of Matthew's Gospel. Using these kinds of categories to judge situations made it hard, on the one hand, to grasp the complexity of real-life situations, and on the other, hindered the Church's ability to offer support and guidance to people using Gospel categories.

In the Synod on the Family this was naturally

a much broader question than the specific issue of the pastoral care of the divorced or separated and remarried and their access to the sacraments, as many believed. Yet the framing of the synod by media linked to particular groups reduced and simplified the whole work of the Synod to this one issue, as if this synod had been called solely to decide whether or not to allow divorced and remarried people to receive Communion. The narrative was set that the Church should either "relax the rules" or maintain its "strict" stance. In other words, the media frame reflecting that narrative reinforced the very casuistry the Synod was seeking to move beyond.

The bad spirit conditioned the discernment, favoring positions on either side ("for" or "against") and encouraging debilitating conflicts. The effect was to reduce the spiritual freedom that is so vital in a synodal process. Each side, entrenched in "their" truth, ended up being imprisoned in their own positions.

Yet the Spirit saved us in the end, in a breakthrough at the close of the second (October 2015) meeting of the Synod on the Family. The overflow, in this case, came above all through those with a deep knowledge of Saint Thomas Aquinas, among them the Archbishop of Vienna, Cardinal Christoph Schönborn. They recovered the true moral doctrine of the authentic scholastic tradition of Saint Thomas, rescuing it from the decadent scholasticism that had led to a casuistic morality.

Because of the immense variety of situations and circumstances people found themselves in, Aquinas's teaching that no general rule could apply in every situation allowed the synod to agree on the need for a case-by-case discernment. There was no need to change the Church's law, only how it was applied. By attending to the specifics of each case, attentive to God's grace operating in the nitty-gritty of people's lives, we could move on from the black-and-white moralism that risked closing off paths of grace and growth. It was neither a tightening nor a loosening of the "rules" but an application of them that left room for circumstances that didn't fit neatly into categories.

This was the great breakthrough the Spirit brought us: a better synthesis of truth and mercy in a fresh understanding drawn from within our own Tradition. Without changing law or doctrine but recovering an authentic meaning of both, the Church is now better able to walk with people who are living together or divorced, to help them see where God's grace is operating in their lives, and to help them embrace the fullness of Church teaching. Chapter 8 of the post-synod document I issued in April 2016, *Amoris Laetitia*, draws on the pure doctrine of Aquinas. Yet it's still hard for some to accept this process: a sign of how many remain not only conditioned by casuistic positions, but also of how their intentions, visions, and even ideologies prevent them from recognizing a synodal path safeguarded by the Church's own Tradition.[21]

In the Synod on Amazonia of October 2019, there was a similar polarization over a secondary issue, but this time without, for now, a resolution by overflow.

The synod was called to highlight the challenges facing the region and its peoples, including the destruction of the rainforest, the murders of indigenous leaders, the marginalization of the indigenous, and the difficulties facing the Church in the region. Yet some people in and through the media again reduced the whole synodal process to the issue of whether or not the Church would be willing to ordain married men, the so-called *viri probati*, even though that question took up a mere three lines in a thirty-page preparatory document.

The fantasy that the synod was "about" this issue minimized and simplified all the region's huge challenges. So that when my apostolic exhortation *Querida Amazonia* came out in February 2020, many felt disappointed or relieved because "the Pope did not open that door." It was as if nobody was interested in the region's ecological, cultural, social, and pastoral dramas; the synod had "failed" because it didn't authorize the ordination of the *viri probati*.

In reality, the synod was a breakthrough in many ways: it gave us a clear mission and a vision to stand with the native peoples, the poor, and the land; and to defend culture and creation against the powerful forces of death and destruction driven solely by profit. It laid the basis for a Church in Amazonia that is deeply embedded in local culture, and with a strong presence of active laypeople; and it set in motion processes such as the creation of the Amazonian bishops' conference. But little of this progress was reported. Amazonia and its peoples were again ignored and silenced, because some media and pressure groups had decided that the synod had been called to resolve one particular issue.

Yet, while there was no resolution of that question, issues came to the fore that I, at least, had not anticipated, and had not been raised in the preparatory document. This is one of the great gifts of the synod process: sometimes the Spirit acts to show us that we are looking in the wrong direction, that what we think the issue is "about" is not. Walking together, listening to what the Spirit has to say to the Church, means allowing for the apparent purity of our positions to be unmasked, and to detect the tares growing among the wheat (Matthew 13:24–30).

An issue that surfaced was the reluctance of

many priests in some of the nine countries that include Amazonia within its borders to be sent as missionaries to the region. They preferred to be sent abroad, to Europe and the United States, where conditions are more comfortable. So the Synod clearly saw a concrete pastoral issue which the bishops of those countries needed to resolve urgently: the lack of solidarity and missionary zeal in the hearts of many of our priests.

In other words, the lack of Sunday celebrations of Mass in some regions—which was the reason given for wanting *viri probati*—was clearly not just due to a lack of ordained ministers, but was also part of a broader lack of missionary commitment to Amazonia. To characterize the issue simply as an absence of available clergy was to conceal a more complex problem.

During the synod assembly itself I saw there were some areas where we can move ahead and yet which are paralyzed. Again, this is a gift of the Spirit in the Synod: to show blockages that are preventing us from taking advantage of the grace of God that is already being offered to us. Why, for example, aren't there enough permanent deacons in the Amazon region? Permanent deacons are vital in reflecting a domestic Church that finds its greatest expression in the Word and in service. In Amazonia a family—a husband and wife, their children—can be a missionary community at the center of a network of relationships.[22]

The Synod showed that to stand with the people, defending their cultures and the natural world, the Church in Amazonia must grow its grassroots presence throughout the region. This can happen only if laypeople are given a decisive role. It is the lay teachers of the faith (catechists) who primarily carry out the task of spreading the Good News of the Gospel, and in the language and customs of the people they serve. That's why I believe it is crucial to trust the lay people, and especially the women who run so many of the communities in the area, to bring forth a distinctively Amazonian holiness that will bear many future fruits. This, in my reading of the synod's discernment, is where the Spirit is pointing.

The danger of becoming trapped in conflict is that we lose perspective. Our horizons shrink and we close off paths the Spirit is showing us. Sometimes walking together means continuing to endure the disagreements, leaving them to be transcended on a higher level at a later time. Time is superior to space and the whole is greater than the parts. This was my own interior discernment, which was confirmed by the discouragement that greeted the exhortation. Let me explain.

Within the synod process, disappointment and a sense of defeat are not signs of the Good Spirit, because they are born of unfulfilled promises, and the Lord always keeps His promises. Outside the synod process, of course, disappointment may be of the Good Spirit, the Lord showing us that a particular path we've chosen is not the right way to go, the kind of disappointment we feel after doing something we thought was enjoyable but later realized was a waste of time or worse. But in the synod process, such disappointment is more likely to reveal an agenda: you came wanting to achieve something, and when you didn't get it, you feel deflated. You may be right (or not), but these are processes that take time, that demand maturity, perseverance, and decision. They call for sowing seeds that others will be able to harvest. In other words, you remain trapped within your desires, rather than allowing yourself to be touched by the grace on offer.

When I hear some say they were disappointed by the Amazonia synod, I think: Didn't we open new pastoral paths? Did the Spirit not show us the need to trust in and allow the growth of a specific church culture in the area that is distinctively lay? For wherever there is a particular need in the Church, the Spirit has already poured out the gifts that can meet it, gifts that need to be received. As *Querida Amazonia* says (#94), we need to be open to bold new possibilities, including the need formally to recognize the remarkable leadership of women in church communities in the region. All of these signs of the Spirit could easily be eclipsed by the narrow focus on the disputed question of broadening the priesthood to include married men.

In walking together, reading the signs of the times, open to the new things of the Spirit, we might take some lessons from this ancient church experience of synodality which I have sought to revive.

First: We need a respectful, mutual listening, free of ideology and predetermined agendas. The aim is not to reach agreement by means of a contest between opposing positions, but to journey together to seek God's will, allowing differences to harmonize. Most important of all is the synodal spirit: to meet each other with respect and trust, to believe in our shared unity, and to receive the new thing that the Spirit wishes to reveal to us.

Second: Sometimes this new thing means resolving disputed questions through overflow. Breakthroughs happen, often at the last minute, leading to a meeting of the minds that allows us to move forward. But the overflow might equally mean an invitation to change our way of thinking and our lenses, to shed our rigidity and our agendas, and look in places we never noticed before. Ours is a God of Surprises, who is always ahead of us.

Third: This is a patient process, which does not come easily to our impatient age. But perhaps, in lockdown, we have learned better how to approach it.

In nineteenth-century Argentina, at a time of frequent wars between strong local governors known as *caudillos*, the story is told of a *caudillo* who was beating a retreat in the midst of a torrential downpour. He gave the order to pitch camp until the skies cleared. But as it was passed from mouth to mouth the order took on a deeper meaning, a wisdom that expressed what his people were living through, wise counsel for times of tribulation and conflict.

Discerning in the midst of conflict requires us sometimes to pitch camp together, waiting for the skies to clear.

Time belongs to the Lord. Trusting in Him, we move forward with courage, building unity through discernment, to discover and implement God's dream for us, and the paths of action ahead.

PART THREE

A TIME TO ACT

In times of crisis and tribulation, when we are shaken out of our sclerotic habits, the love of God comes out to purify us, to remind us that we are a people. Once we were not a people; but now we are God's people (1 Peter 2:10). The closeness of God calls us together. "Thou hast made me known to friends whom I knew not," writes the poet Rabindranath Tagore. "Thou hast brought the distant near and made a brother of the stranger."[23] This time for action asks us to recover our sense of belonging, the knowledge that we are part of a people.

What does it mean, to be "a people"? It is a thought category, a mythical concept, not in the sense of a fantasy or a fable but as a particular story that makes a universal truth tangible and visible. The mythical category of the "people" draws on and expresses many sources: historic, linguistic, cultural (especially in music and dance), but above all a collective wisdom and memory. A people is held together by that memory, treasured in history, custom, rites (religious or not), and other bonds that transcend the purely transactional and rational.

At the beginning of the story of every people is a quest for dignity and freedom, a history of solidarity and struggle. For the people of Israel, it was the exodus from their slavery in Egypt. For the Romans, it was the foundation of a city. For the nations of the American continent, it was the struggle for independence.

Just as a people comes to an awareness of its shared dignity in times of struggle, in war and hardship, so, too, a people can forget that awareness. A people can become oblivious to its own history. In times of peace and prosperity, there is always the risk that the people might dissolve into a mere mass, with no unifying principle to bind them.

When this happens, the center lives at the expense of the margins, people divide into competing tribes, and the exploited and disrespected might burn with resentment at the injustices. Rather than thinking of ourselves as members of a people, we have competition for dominance, turning contrapositions into contradictions. Because, in these circumstances, the people no longer see the natural world as their inheritance to be nurtured; the powerful seize and extract all they can from it, while putting nothing back. Indifference, egotism, a culture of complacent well-being, and deep divisions within society, spilling out into violence—all these are signs that a people has lost awareness of its dignity. It has ceased to believe in itself.

A people thus weakened and divided easily falls prey to very different kinds of colonization. But even when not occupied by a foreign power, the people has, in a larger sense, already surrendered its dignity. It has ceased to be a protagonist of its own history.

Every now and then, however, great calamities awaken the memory of that original liberation and unity. Prophets who have sought to recall the people to what really matters, to its first love, suddenly find eager audiences. Times of tribulation offer the possibility that what oppresses the people—both internally and externally—can be overthrown, and a new age of freedom begin.

Such calamities for a time throw us off balance, yet, paradoxically, they can allow a people to recover its memory, and therefore its capacity for action, its hope. Crisis has shown that our peoples are not subject to blind forces but in adversity are capable of acting. Calamities unmask our shared vulnerability and expose those false, superfluous securities around which we had organized our plans, routines, and priorities. They reveal our neglect of what nourishes and strengthens the life of the community, how we had shriveled within our bubbles of indifference and well-being. We learn that in our restlessness and frustration, in our fascination with new things, in craving recognition in manic busyness, we had failed to pay attention to the suffering all around us.

In their response to that suffering is measured the authentic character of our peoples.

As we awaken to the memory of our people's dignity, we start to grasp the insufficiency of the pragmatic categories which have replaced the mythical category that gave us our true way of life. The people of Israel in the desert preferred the pure pragmatism of a golden calf to the freedom to which the Lord called them. In the same way we had been told that society is just an amalgam of individuals each pursuing their own best interests; that the unity of the people is mere fable; that we are powerless before the might of the market and the state; and that life's purpose is profit and power.

But now, come the storm, we see that it is not so.

We must not let the current clarifying moment pass us by. Let it not be said, in years to come, that in response to the coronavirus crisis we failed to act to restore the dignity of our peoples, to recover our memory and to remember our roots.

The term "the people" can have contrasting connotations in our different languages. Exploited by ideologies and harnessed to sectarian politics, it can have overtones of totalitarianism or class struggle. In our own day it is deployed in the exclusionary rhetoric of populism. So it would help to explain what *I* mean by "the people."

A people is not the same as a country, a nation,

or a state, important though these entities are. A country is a geographical entity; the nation-state is the juridical and constitutional scaffolding that gives it force. But these boundaries and structures can change. A country that has been amputated or lost a war can remake itself. A nation that undergoes a constitutional crisis can rebuild itself. But to lose the feeling of being part of a people is very hard to recover from. It is a loss that takes place over decades, eroding our capacity for encounter. As the reference points we inherited from our forebears fade, so we lose our capacity to come together as a people to create a better future.

The feeling of being part of a people can only be recovered in the same way as it was forged: in shared struggle and hardship. The people is always the fruit of a synthesis, of an encounter, of a fusion of disparate elements that generates a whole which is greater than its parts. A people may have profound disagreements and differences, but they can walk together inspired by shared goals, and so create a future. Classically, a people gathers itself in assemblies and organizes. It shares experiences and hopes, and it hears the call of a common destiny.

In Argentina we speak of the ingenuity of the people, meaning its historic ability to identify paths ahead, to "sniff out" solutions to current problems. To know ourselves as a people is to be aware of something greater that unites us, something that cannot be reduced to a shared legal or physical identity. We saw this in the protests in reaction to the killing of George Floyd, when many people who otherwise did not know each other took to the streets to protest, united by a healthy indignation. Such moments reveal not just popular feeling but the feeling of a people, its "soul." For in spite of the constant social erosions, there persists in all peoples reserves of fundamental values: the struggle for life from conception to natural death, the defense of human dignity, a love of freedom, a concern for justice and creation, the love of family and *fiesta*.

It may seem strange to say it, but it's true: the people has a soul. And because we can speak of the soul of a people, we can speak of a way of viewing the world, an awareness. Such an awareness is the result not of an economic system or political theory but of a personality shaped in key moments of a people's history. These milestones have imprinted on the people a powerful sense of solidarity, of justice, and of the importance of labor.

When the people prays, what does it ask for? For health, work, family, school; for a decent place to live; for enough money to get by; for peace between neighbors, and a fresh chance for the poor. These aims may not seem revolutionary or high-minded. But the people itself knows all too well that they are the fruit of justice.

A people, then, is not merely the sum of individuals. It is neither a logical nor a legal category, but a living reality that is the fruit of a shared integrating principle. You can try to describe the people as a concept, in terms of a paradigm, to try to define where it begins or ends, or to impose some legal or rational definition of it. And you can analyze a particular people in terms of its culture or characteristics, to try to name what defines, say, the French or the American people. But ultimately the exercise is futile. To make the people a topic of research is to put yourself outside it, and in so doing, to lose sight of what it is. Because "the people" is not a logical concept, it can really only be approached through intuition, by entering into its spirit, its heart, its history and traditions.

The people is a category capable of generating symphony out of disconnection, of harmonizing difference while preserving distinctiveness. To speak of the people is to offer an antidote to the perennial temptation of creating elites, whether intellectual, moral, religious, political, economic, or cultural. Elitism reduces and restricts the riches that the Lord placed on the earth, turning them into possessions to be exploited by some rather than gifts to be shared. Enlightened elites always end the same way, imposing their criteria, and in the process scorning and excluding all those who do not conform to their social status, moral stature, or ideology. We have suffered for too long from these reductionisms.

To speak of a people is to appeal to unity in diversity: *e pluribus unum.* For example, the twelve tribes of Israel were gathered into one people, harmonized around a common axis (Deuteronomy 26:5) yet without giving up the distinctive characteristics of each one. The People of God, in this case, takes up the tensions which are normal in any human grouping, but without needing to resolve them by one element prevailing over the others.

I realize that explaining this thought category is not easy, not least because we have become so used to speaking of identity in categories of exclusion and differentiation. That is why I prefer to use the archetypal term "mythical category," for it opens up a different way of describing reality, one that allows us to forge an identity that is not determined by exclusion and differentiation and dialectical opposition, but through the synthesis of potentialities that I call overflow.

If, faced with the challenge not just of this pandemic but of all the ills that afflict us at this time, we can act as a single people, life and society will change for the better. This is not just an idea but a call to each of us, an invitation to abandon the self-defeating isolation of individualism, to flow out from my own "little lagoon" into the broad river of a reality and destiny of which I am part yet which at the same time lie beyond me.

When I speak of *the dignity of the people,* I mean this awareness that arises from the people's "soul," from its way of looking at the world. Where does that dignity come from? Does it stem from a people's wealth, its victories in war? Such achievements may be the source of pride, or even arrogance. But the dignity of a people—even the poorest, most wretched, enslaved people— comes from God's closeness. It is God's love and closeness that confer dignity, and always raise up a people, offering it a horizon of hope. In this sense it is good to look to the people of Israel and its people, the archetype of what we are discussing.

The Bible tells this story over and over. In calling Moses, God saves a people by manifesting His closeness, pledging Himself to them in an eternal covenant of love. Summoning Abraham, God promises to walk with His people, to be near to them. Aware of God's dedication to them, the Jewish people becomes conscious of its dignity and can move ahead, caring for its poor, building strong institutions, and achieving a nobility of soul. But when it loses that awareness—when

Israel abandons the law of the Lord, which is the gift of God's closeness (2 Chronicles 12:1)—it collapses into schism and injustice.

When Saint Paul is asked to explain his faith in Jesus Christ, he recounts the whole history of divine closeness to the people (Acts 13:13–21), as does Stephen before his martyrdom (Acts 7:1–54). Jesus Christ, the anointed of God, is part of that story of a people's salvation, a salvation he extends to all. Hence the Second Vatican Council described the Church as the "People of God," a people anointed with the grace of the Holy Spirit, incarnate in all the peoples of this earth, each with its own culture—a people with many faces.

Jesus is a child of the Jewish people's history of grace, of promise, of redemption. His is a story of a people seeking liberation, conscious of its dignity because God has appeared and come close and walked with them. Jesus comes to restore Israel to the remembrance of God's closeness, to return to the people the dignity of the promise. Without that consciousness of its dignity, Roman occupation or not, the people will remain enslaved.

Jesus restores dignity to the people in acts and words that perform God's closeness. No one is saved alone. Isolation is not part of our faith. God attracts us within a complex web of relationships and sends us out into the middle of the crossroads of history.

To be Christian, then, is to know that we are part of a people, a people expressed in different nations and cultures yet which transcends all boundaries of race and language. The People of God is a community within the broader community of a nation, serving the nation, helping to shape that nation's self-understanding, while respecting the role played by other religious and cultural institutions. But if the Church has a particular role to play at times of crisis, it is precisely to remind the people of its soul, of its need to respect the common good. This is what Jesus did: He came to strengthen and deepen the bonds of belonging—of the people to God and to each other. That is why the one who matters most in the Kingdom of God is whoever makes himself least, serving others (Matthew 20:26–27), and especially the poor.

The Church is a people with many faces, and expresses this truth in countless different ways, according to each culture. That is why I like to think that evangelization must always be in the dialect of each place, with the same words and sounds that a grandmother uses to sing lullabies to her grandchildren.

The Church is called to be the People of God incarnated within a history, in a concrete place, in the language of that place. At the same time, God's people and the mission of Jesus transcend all boundaries of culture and geography. The

Church's mission is directed to the People of God; and yet part of its task is to remind a nation that there is a common good of humanity which supersedes that of any particular people. The whole is always greater than the parts, and unity must transcend conflict.

This is why a Christian will always defend individual rights and freedoms but can never be an individualist. A Christian will love and serve her country with patriotic feeling, but cannot be merely a nationalist.

The firm center of Christianity is the essential proclamation, the *kerygma*. It means that God loved me and gave himself up for me. The death and resurrection of Jesus Christ, His love on the Cross, are what calls us to be missionary disciples, inviting us to recognize each other as brothers and sisters of the larger human family, and especially of those who feel themselves orphans. As the Beatitudes and Matthew chapter 25 show us, the principle of salvation is fulfilled in the compassion we demonstrate.

In this sense the Bible offers us a clear contrast between the indifference of Cain toward the fate of Abel—"Am I my brother's keeper?" (Genesis 4:9)—and the response of Yahweh to Moses in the third chapter of Exodus: "I have observed the misery of my people . . . I have heard their cry . . . and I have come down to deliver them" (Exodus 3:7–8). One is the way of non-belonging; the other way is involvement in the life of a people and a determination to serve and save.

That is why the Church must always be known for its closeness to the peoples of this earth in their struggle for dignity and freedom. In each culture where it is present, the Church must see people's sorrows and its hopes—and especially those of the poorest—as its own. The Church walks as part of the people, serving it, not trying to organize it in paternalistic fashion, because a people organizes itself.

If you were to ask me what is one of the ways Christianity has gone astray, I would not hesitate: it is to *forget that we belong to a people*. As Father Zossima says in *The Brothers Karamazov*: "salvation will come from the people."[24] To set yourself above the People of God is to ignore that the Lord has already come close to His people, anointing them, raising them up.

Setting oneself above the people leads to moralism, legalism, clericalism, pharisaism, and other elitist ideologies, which know nothing of the joy of knowing yourself to be part of God's people. The Church's role is played out in the service of the Lord and the peoples of the earth where she is sent, not by imposing or dominating but as Christ does, in the washing of feet.

The current crisis calls us to recover our sense of belonging; only thus will our peoples again be subjects of their own history.

This is the time to restore an ethics of fraternity and solidarity, regenerating the bonds of trust and belonging. For what saves us is not an idea but an encounter. Only the face of another is capable of awakening the best of ourselves. In serving the people, we save ourselves.

If we are to come out of this crisis better, we have to recover the knowledge that as a people we have a shared destination. The pandemic has reminded us that no one is saved alone.

What ties us to each other is what we commonly call solidarity. Solidarity is more than acts of generosity, important as these are; it is the call to embrace the reality that we are bound by bonds of reciprocity. On this solid foundation we can build a better, different, human future.

It is an understanding sadly absent from contemporary political narratives, whether liberal or populist. The dominant worldview of Western politics views society as merely an aggregate of coexisting interests, and is suspicious of language that values the bonds of community and culture. On the other hand we have worldviews—such as the various kinds of populism—that deform the meaning of the word "people" by hitching it to ideologies that focus on perceived enemies, internal and external. If one worldview exalts and promotes the atomized individual, leaving little room for fraternity and solidarity, the other reduces the people to a faceless mass it claims to represent.

It is striking how neoliberal currents of thought have sought to exclude from the political arena any substantive debate about the common good and the universal destination of goods.[25] What they promote instead is essentially the efficient management of a market and minimal government control. But the problem is that when the economy's primary purpose centers on profit, it is easy to forget that the earth's resources are for all, not the few.

The obsession with profit weakens the institutions that can protect a people from reckless economic interests and the excessive concentration of power. The increasing social conflicts are in large part fed by inequality and injustice, but their underlying cause lies in the fraying of the bonds of belonging. An atomized society can never be at peace with itself because it fails to see the social effects of inequality. Fraternity is today our new frontier.

When they conceive of the individual exclusively in relation to the state and the market, as a radically autonomous individual, liberal movements view institutions and traditions with suspicion. Yet there exists, often in hidden ways, an instinct—if we can call it that—by which most of us remain deeply drawn to family, community, and the history of our people. It is in the mediating institutions of society—beginning with the family—rather than the market that people find meaning in their lives, where they learn the dimensions of trust and solidarity. Which is why I am concerned about a certain kind of media culture that seeks to uproot especially the younger generations from their richest traditions, stripping them of their history, their culture, and their religious heritage. An uprooted person is very easy to dominate.

Religious and other convictions offer unique insights on the world; they are sources of good. They generate convictions—of solidarity and service—that can strengthen society as a whole. They are places of reconciliation where people experience what the market will never be able to give them: their worth as people, rather than just their value as employees or consumers.

Brought together in the kinds of synod-type dialogue we explored in the second part of this book, people in different institutions and diverse convictions are able to produce surprising harmonies. Disagreements of a philosophical or theological nature—between faiths, or between secular groups and people of faith—are not obstacles to uniting to pursue shared goals, as long as everyone involved shares a concern for the common good. Rigidity and fundamentalism can be found in some institutions, it is true, but they usually do not engage in this kind of dialogue.

• • •

The laissez-faire market-centered approach confuses ends and means. Rather than being seen as a source of dignity, work becomes merely a means of production; profit turns into a goal rather than a means to achieving greater goods. From here we can end up subscribing to the tragically mistaken belief that whatever is good for the market is good for society.

I don't criticize the market per se. I decry the all-too-common scenario where ethics and the economy have been decoupled. And I criticize the self-evidently fictitious idea that wealth must be allowed to roam unhindered in order to deliver prosperity for all. The refutation of that idea is all around us: left to their own devices, markets have generated vast inequality and huge ecological damage. Once capital becomes an idol that presides over a socioeconomic system, it enslaves us, sets us at odds with each other, excludes the poor, and endangers the planet we all share. Little wonder that Basil of Caesarea, one of the Church's first theologians, called money "the devil's dung."

Thus, a neoliberal economy ends up with no real objective other than growth. Yet market forces cannot on their own deliver the goal we now need: to regenerate the natural world by living more sustainably and more soberly while meeting the needs of those who have been harmed by or excluded from that economy until now. Unless we accept the principle of solidarity among the peoples, we will not come out of this crisis better.

The market is an instrument for exchanging and circulating goods, for building relationships that allow us to grow and thrive, and for expanding our opportunities. But markets do not govern themselves. They need to be underpinned by laws and regulations that ensure they work for the common good. The free market is anything but free for huge numbers of people, above all for the poor, who end up with little or no choice in practice. That is why Saint John Paul II spoke of a "social" market economy: including the term "social" allows for an opening up to the community dimension.

When I speak of solidarity I mean much more than the promotion of philanthropic works or financial assistance to help those who lose out. Because solidarity is not the sharing of crumbs from the table, but to make space at the table for everyone. The dignity of the people calls for communion: for the sharing and multiplying of goods, and for the participation of all for the sake of all.

The issue that must be confronted is human fragility, the inclination to close ourselves off in our own narrow interests. That is why we need an economy with goals beyond the narrow focus on growth, that puts human dignity, jobs, and ecological regeneration at its core. The dignity of our peoples demands an economy that doesn't merely enable the accumulation of goods, but allows all to access good work, housing, education, and health.

In the absence of social goals, "profit-first" economic growth has fed a crony capitalism that serves not the common good but speculators in the "liquid economy." Collateral banking systems, offshore sites providing fiscal havens for corporate tax avoidance, extracting value from companies to boost the earnings of shareholders at the expense of stakeholders, the smoke-and-mirrors world of derivatives and credit default swaps—all these suck capital from the real economy and undermine a healthy market, creating historically unprecedented levels of inequality.

There is today a major disjuncture between the awareness of social rights on the one hand and the distribution of actual opportunities on the other. The stupendous rise in inequality of recent decades is not a stage of growth but a brake on it, and the root of many social ills in the twenty-first century. Barely more than one percent of the world's population owns half of its wealth. A market ever more detached from morality, dazzled by its own complex engineering, which privileges profit and competition above all else, means not just spectacular wealth for a few but also poverty and deprivation for many. Millions are robbed of hope.

Too often we have thought of society as a subset of the economy and democracy as a function of the market. It is time to restore their proper order, to find the means to guarantee a life for all worthy of being called human. We need to set goals for our business sector that—without denying its importance—look beyond shareholder value to other kinds of values that save us all: community, nature, and meaningful work. Profits are a sign of a business's health, but we need broader measures of profit that take into account social and environmental goals.

Similarly, we need a vision of politics that isn't just about managing the apparatus of the state and campaigning for reelection but is capable of cultivating virtue and forging new bonds. We need to rehabilitate Politics with a capital P, as I like to call it, as a service to the common good. It is a vocation above all for those disturbed by the state of society and the plight of the poorest.

We need politicians who burn with the mission to secure for their people the three Ls of land, lodging, and labor, as well as education and health care. That means politicians with broader horizons who can open new ways for the people to organize and express itself. It means politicians who serve the people rather than who make use of them, who walk with those they represent, who carry with them the smell of the neighborhoods they serve. This kind of politics will be the best antidote to corruption in all its forms.

Our age calls for a class of politicians and leaders who take inspiration from Jesus's parable of the Good Samaritan, which shows how we can develop our lives, our calling and mission. So often what we find at the bottom of it all is the issue of distance. Faced with the man left at the side of the road, some decide to walk on: distant from the situation, they prefer to ignore the facts and carry on as if nothing had happened. Imprisoned in various kinds of thinking and justifications, they pass on by.

It's the same problem as ever: poverty conceals itself in shame. In order to see, understand, and feel it, you have to come close. You can't know poverty from a distance; you have to touch it. To recognize and come close—that's the first step. The second step consists in responding practically and immediately, because a concrete act of mercy is always an act of justice.

But a third step is necessary if we are not to fall into mere welfarism: to reflect on the first two steps and open ourselves to the necessary structural reforms. An authentic politics designs those changes alongside, with, and by means of all those affected, respecting their culture and their dignity. The only time it is right to look down at someone is when we are offering our hand to help them get up. As I once put it in a talk to some religious men and women: "The problem is not feeding the poor, or clothing the naked, or visiting the sick, but rather recognizing that the poor, the naked, the sick, prisoners, and the homeless have the dignity to sit at our table, to feel 'at home' among us, to feel part of a family. This is the sign that the Kingdom of Heaven is in our midst."[26]

In the post-Covid world, neither technocratic managerialism nor populism will suffice. Only a politics rooted in the people, open to the people's own organization, will be able to change our future.

When the accumulation of wealth becomes our chief goal, whether as individuals or as an economy, we practice a form of idolatry that puts us in chains. It is inconceivable that so many women and children are being exploited for power, pleasure, or profit. Our brothers and sisters are being enslaved in clandestine warehouses, exploited as undocumented migrants and in prostitution rings, and the situation is even worse when it is children subject to such injustices, all for profit and the greed of a few.

Human trafficking is often tied to other global plagues—trafficking in arms and drugs, the trade in wildlife and organs—which degrade our world. These vast networks generating hundreds of billions of dollars cannot survive without the complicity of powerful people. States would seem to be powerless to act. Only a new kind of politics, which partners state resources with organizations and institutions rooted in civil society close to the problem, can rise to these challenges.

The dignity of our peoples demands safe corridors for migrants and refugees so they can move without fear from deadly areas to safer ones. It is unacceptable to deter immigration by letting hundreds of migrants die in perilous sea crossings or desert treks. The Lord will ask us to account for each one of those deaths.

Lockdown opened our eyes to a reality that is so often hidden: the basic needs of the most developed societies are being met by poorly paid migrants, yet they are scapegoated and denigrated, and denied the right to safe and decent work. Migration is a global issue. No one should be obliged to flee their country. But the wrong is doubled when the migrant is forced into the hands of people traffickers in order to cross borders; and tripled when they reach the land they thought would give them a better future, only to find themselves despised, exploited, abandoned, or enslaved. We need to welcome, promote, protect, and integrate those who come in search of better lives for themselves and their families. Of course, governments need prudently to assess their ability to welcome and integrate.

Both slavery and the death penalty were once deemed acceptable, even in societies considered Christian. Today the Christian conscience benefits from a deeper understanding of the sanctity of life that has grown over time. Both slavery and capital punishment are unacceptable, yet both continue: the first clandestinely, the second quite openly as part of the judicial systems of some developed countries, where even Christians try to justify it. But as I said in the U.S. Congress in 2015: "A just and necessary punishment must never exclude the dimension of hope and the goal of rehabilitation."[27]

While many will be irritated to hear a pope return to the topic, I cannot stay silent over 30 to 40 million unborn lives cast aside every year through abortion.[28] It is painful to behold how in many regions that see themselves as developed the practice is often urged because the children to come are disabled, or unplanned.

Human life is never a burden. It demands we make space for it, not cast it off. Of course the arrival of a new human life in need—whether the unborn child in the womb or the migrant at our border—challenges and changes our priorities. With abortion and closed borders we refuse that readjustment of our priorities, sacrificing human life to defend our economic security or to assuage our fear that parenthood will upend our lives. Abortion is a grave injustice. It can never be a legitimate expression of autonomy and power. If our autonomy demands the death of another, it is none other than an iron cage. I often ask myself these two questions: Is it right to eliminate a human life to resolve a problem? Is it right to hire an assassin to resolve a problem?

The neo-Darwinist ideology of the survival of the fittest, underpinned by an unfettered market obsessed with profit and individual sovereignty, has penetrated our culture and hardened our hearts. The successful growth of the technocratic paradigm so often demands the sacrifice of innocent lives: the child abandoned in the streets; the underage sweatshop worker who rarely sees the light of day; the worker dismissed because his company has been asset-stripped to generate dividends for shareholders; the refugees denied the chance to work; the elderly abandoned to their fate in underfunded care homes.

My predecessor Saint Paul VI warned in his 1968 encyclical letter *Humanae Vitae* of the temptation to view human life as one more object over which the powerful and educated should exercise mastery. How prophetic his message now looks! These days, prenatal diagnosis is commonly used to filter out those deemed weak or inferior, while at the other end of life, euthanasia is becoming normal: either overtly, through assisted suicide laws in some countries or states, or covertly, through neglect of the elderly.

The deeper causes of this erosion of the value of life have to be faced. By excluding from public policymaking any consideration of the common good, one ends up promoting individual autonomy to the exclusion of all other values and reference points. Without a vision for society rooted in the dignity of all people, the logic of the unfettered market ends up turning life from a gift into a product.

There is a twelfth-century biblical *midrash*, or commentary, on the story of the Tower of Babel in chapter 11 of the Book of Genesis. The tower was a monument to the ego of the people of Babel. Building the tower required huge numbers of bricks, which were very expensive to make. According to the rabbi, if a brick fell it was a great tragedy: work stopped and the negligent worker was beaten severely as an example. But if a worker fell to his death? The work went on. One of the surplus laborers—slaves waiting in line for work—stepped forward to take his place so that the tower could continue to rise.

Which was more valuable, the brick or the worker? Which was considered an expendable surplus in the pursuit of endless growth?

And nowadays? When shares of major

corporations fall a few percent, the news makes headlines. Experts endlessly discuss what it might mean. But when a homeless person is found frozen in the streets behind empty hotels, or a whole population goes hungry, few notice; and if it makes the news at all, we just shake our heads sadly and carry on, believing there is no solution.

This is what Jesus meant when he said you cannot serve both God and money. In our lives, just as in our societies, if you put money at the center, you enter the pattern of sacrifice: whatever the human cost or the damage to the environment, the tower must go higher and higher. But when you put people's dignity at the center, you create a new logic of mercy and of care. Then what is truly of value is restored to its rightful place.

Either a society is geared to a culture of sacrifice—the triumph of the fittest and the throwaway culture—or to mercy and care. People or bricks: it is time to choose.

Behind the rise of populist politics in recent years is a genuine anguish: many feel thrust aside by the ruthless juggernaut of globalized technocracy. Populisms are often described as a protest against globalization, although they are more properly a protest against the globalization of indifference. At bottom they reflect pain at the loss of roots and community, and a generalized feeling of anguish. Yet, in generating fear and sowing panic, populisms are the exploitation of that popular anguish, not its remedy. The often cruel rhetoric of populist leaders denigrating the "other" in order to defend a national or group identity reveals its spirit. It is a means by which ambitious politicians attain power.

Today, listening to some of the populist leaders we now have, I am reminded of the 1930s, when some democracies collapsed into dictatorships seemingly overnight. By turning the people into a category of exclusion—threatened on all sides by enemies, internal and external—the term was emptied of meaning. We see it happening again now in rallies where populist leaders excite and harangue crowds, channeling their resentments and hatreds against imagined enemies to distract from the real problems.

In the name of the people, populism denies the proper participation of those who belong to the people, allowing a particular group to appoint itself the true interpreter of popular feeling. A people ceases to be a people and becomes an inert mass manipulated by a party or a demagogue. Dictatorships almost always begin this way: sowing fear in the hearts of the people, then offering to defend them from the object of their fear in exchange for denying them the power to determine their own future.

For example, a fantasy of national-populism in countries with Christian majorities is its defense of "Christian civilization" from perceived enemies, whether Islam, Jews, the European Union, or the United Nations. The defense appeals to those who are often no longer religious but who regard their nation's inheritance as a kind of identity. Their fears and loss of identity have increased at the same time as attendance at churches has declined.

The loss of relationship with God and a loss of a sense of universal fraternity have contributed to this sense of isolation and fear of the future. Thus irreligious or superficially religious people vote for populists to protect their religious identity, unconcerned that fear and hatred of the other cannot be reconciled with the Gospel.

The heart of Christianity is God's love for all peoples and our love for our neighbors, especially those in need. To reject a struggling migrant, whatever his or her religious belief, out of fear of diluting a "Christian" culture is grotesquely to mispresent both Christianity and culture. Migration is not a threat to Christianity except in the minds of those who benefit from claiming it is. To promote the Gospel and not welcome the strangers in need, nor affirm their humanity as children of God, is to seek to encourage a culture that is Christian in name only, emptied of all that makes it distinctive.

• • •

To recover the dignity of the people we need to go to the margins of our societies to meet all those who live there. Hidden there are ways of looking at the world that can give us all a fresh start. We cannot dream of the future while continuing to ignore the lives of practically a third of the world's population rather than seeing them as a resource.

I mean those who lack regular work living on the margins of the market economy. They are landless peasants and smallholders, subsistence fishermen and sweatshop workers, garbage pickers and street vendors, sidewalk artisans, slum dwellers and squatters. In developed countries, they are the ones who live from odd jobs, often on the move, poorly housed, with poor access to drinking water and healthy food: both they and their families suffer all kinds of vulnerability.

Yet if we manage to come close and put aside our stereotypes we discover that many of them are far from being merely passive victims. Organized in a global archipelago of associations and movements, they represent the hope of solidarity in an age of exclusion and indifference. On the margins I have discovered so many social movements with roots in parishes or schools that bring people together to make them become protagonists of their own histories, to set in

158

motion dynamics that smacked of dignity. Taking life as it comes, they do not sit around resigned or complaining but come together to convert injustice into new possibilities. I call them "social poets." In mobilizing for change, in their search for dignity, I see a source of moral energy, a reserve of civic passion, capable of revitalizing our democracy and reorienting the economy.

It was precisely here that the Church was born, in the margins of the Cross where so many of the crucified are found. If the Church disowns the poor, she ceases to be the Church of Jesus; she falls back on the old temptation to become a moral or intellectual elite. There is only one word for the Church that becomes a stranger to the poor: "scandal." The road to the geographic and existential margins is the route of the Incarnation: God chose the peripheries as the place to reveal, in Jesus, His saving action in history.

This is what led me to walk with the Popular Movements. Hosting leaders of more than a hundred of these at the Vatican at meetings in 2014 and 2016, and in Santa Cruz, Bolivia, in July 2015, I addressed them and could dialogue with them. These World Meetings, as they became known, focused on the need to give people access to land, lodging, and labor, which in Spanish we call the "three Ts": *tierra, techo, trabajo.*[29]

I wrote to the leaders of the Popular Movements

during lockdown to express my closeness and to encourage them. I knew that, not only were they excluded from the chance to work, but because they worked in the informal economy they were beyond the reach of government measures to protect citizens' jobs and livelihoods. I described them as an "invisible army" on the front lines of this pandemic, an army with only the weapons of solidarity, hope, and a sense of community, working tirelessly for their families, neighborhoods, and the common good.[30]

To be clear: this is not the Church "organizing" the people. These are organizations that already exist—some Christian, some not. I would like the Church to open its doors more widely to these movements; I hope every diocese in the world has an ongoing collaboration with them, as some already do. But my role and that of the Church is to accompany, not paternalize them. That means offering teaching and guidance, but never imposing doctrine or trying to control them. The Church illuminates with the light of the Gospel, awakening the peoples to their own dignity, but it is the people who have the instinct to organize themselves.

My conviction that these people's movements are generating something powerful comes from my time as archbishop in Buenos Aires. After I got to know an organization working to free victims of human trafficking and other forms of modern slavery, I celebrated a large outdoor Mass in the Plaza Constitución each July specifically for exploited people on the margins of society. Over time these Masses became a gathering place for thousands who came to pray, to ask God for things they needed.

I felt the Good Spirit there, in that prayerful crowd. I don't mean "crowd" in the impersonal sense of a mass of people. Nor do I mean the kind of organization which thinks and talks on behalf of the poor, but rather the People of God coming together to pray for the pain of their sons and daughters. This crowd gathered in prayer reminded the city of what it no longer mourned: the normalization of sin, the sufferings of so many. The lead voice in that crowd was the voice of the Holy Spirit seeking to renew the prophecy which as a Church we cannot ever silence.

It is not the Church's task to organize every action of the people but rather to encourage, walk with, and support those who carry out these roles. Which is quite the opposite of how elites of all kinds think—"All for the people, but nothing with the people," whom they suppose to be faceless and ignorant.

It is not true. A people knows what it wants and needs, and has an instinct.

In Plaza Constitución, I met a crowd that reminded me of the crowd that followed the

Lord: the ordinary people who would stay for hours listening to Jesus until evening fell and they didn't know what to do. The crowd that followed Jesus was not a mass of individuals hypnotized by some deft orator, but a people with a history, with a hope, who safeguarded a promise.

The people always hold in their hearts a promise: an invitation that leads them toward what they desire, despite the exclusion they suffer. Jesus's preaching evoked in them ancient promises they carried in their guts, in their blood: an ancestral awareness of God's closeness and of their own dignity. By bringing to them that closeness in the way He spoke and touched and healed, Jesus showed that awareness was real. He opened for them a path of hope into the future, a path of liberation that was not merely political but something more: a human liberation, that conferred that dignity that only the Lord can give us.

That's why they followed Jesus. He gave them dignity. In that powerful scene of Jesus alone with the woman caught in adultery, after her accusers have gone from the scene, Jesus anoints her with dignity, and tells her: "Go your way, and from now on do not sin again" (John 8:11). For Jesus, every person is capable of dignity and has value. Jesus restores the true worth of each person and of the people as a whole because He can see with God's eyes: "God saw that it was good" (Genesis 1:10).

To do this Jesus had to reject the mindset of the religious elites of his day, who had taken ownership of law and tradition. Possession of the goods of religion became a means of putting themselves above others, others not like them, whom they inspected and judged. By mixing with tax collectors and "women of ill repute," Jesus wrested religion from its imprisonment in the confines of the elites, of specialized knowledge and of privileged families, in order to make every person and situation capable of God (*capax Dei*). By walking with the poor, the outcasts, and the marginalized, He smashed the wall that prevented the Lord from coming close to His people, among His flock.

In showing God's closeness to the poor and sinners, Jesus indicted the mindset that trusts in self-justification, ignoring what happens around them. Jesus challenges the mindset that, at its worst, leads to the use of racist terms, denigrating those who do not belong to a particular group, which portrays migrants as a threat and builds walls to dominate and exclude.

What I saw in the people who gathered in Constitution Square was the crowd that followed Jesus: they were dignified and they were organized. They carried within them the dignity that God's closeness had revealed to them.

Among them were the *cartoneros*, the men and boys who scour the streets at night in search of cardboard and other materials that they sell to recyclers. The *cartoneros* had appeared as a result of Argentina's economic collapse of 2001–2002, often found pulling their huge bags with the material they had collected along the streets. I remember one night seeing a cart being pulled by what I assumed was a horse, but when I got closer I saw it was two boys, younger than twelve years old. City laws banned animal-drawn transport, so apparently a child was worth less than a horse.

Over time the tens of thousands of *cartoneros*, with their sense of dignity, organized and secured rights to pay and protection. You might think: that is what trade unions are for. Normally trade unions focus on workers in formal employment, offering them their protection and helping maintain decent jobs. But, sadly, nowadays few unions look out for those on the margins. Many are remote from the edges of society.

After I got to know the *cartoneros*, I joined them one night as they made their rounds. I went dressed in civilian clothing and without my bishop's pectoral cross; only the leaders knew who I was. I saw how they worked, how they lived off the city's leftovers, recycling what society discarded, and I saw, too, how some elites regarded them as leftovers themselves. Moving

164

at night through the city with them, I could see the city through their eyes and experience the indifference they suffered, that indifference that turns into a well-mannered, silent violence.

I saw the face of the throwaway culture. But I also saw the dignity of the *cartoneros*: how hard they worked to maintain their families and feed their children, how they worked collaboratively, as a community. In organizing they entered into their own kind of conversion, a recycling of their own lives. And along the way they changed the way Argentines viewed their garbage, helping them to understand the value of reusing and recycling.

I'm not idealizing the *cartoneros*: they have fights and conflicts and some who try to take advantage of others, just as you get at every level of society. But I was moved by their solidarity and hospitality: how, when one of them was in need, they joined together for the sake of the person's family. The *cartoneros* were an example of people on the margins organizing to survive, and exemplifying the dignity that is the mark of people's movements.

When those who are cast aside organize for the sake not of an ideology or to gain power but to achieve access to the three Ls of a dignified life—land, lodging, and labor—for their families, we can say that here is a sign, a promise, and a prophecy. This is why, as Pope, I've encouraged and walked with the Popular Movements around the world, addressing, for example, a meeting in Modesto, California, in February 2017, organized by the U.S. bishops' conference and PICO, a national network of community organizations.

At each meeting I've given the message that reversing the processes of dehumanization in our current world will depend on the participation of the people's movements. They are sowers of a new future, promoters of the change we need: to put the economy at the service of the people, to build peace and justice, and to defend Mother Earth.

The health of a society can be judged by its periphery. A periphery that is abandoned, sidelined, despised, and neglected shows an unstable, unhealthy society that cannot long survive without major reforms. But to quote Hölderlin again: "Where the danger is, also grows the saving power." From the edges comes the hope of restoring the dignity of the people. That is true not just of the margins of poverty and need, but of all the margins created by religious or ideological persecution and other kinds of brutality. By opening up to the margins, to the people's organizations, we unleash change.

To embrace the margins is to expand our horizons, for we see more clearly and broadly from the edges of society. We need to recover the wisdom hidden in our neighborhoods which the people's movements make visible. It is a mistake to dismiss the Popular Movements as "little" and "local"; that would be to miss their vitality and relevance. They have the potential to revitalize our societies, rescuing them from all that today weakens them.

The meetings of the Popular Movements at the Vatican and elsewhere allowed for the creation of an agenda for change they had been developing for a while. They made the case for a lifestyle that rejects consumerism and recovers the value of life, solidarity, and respect for nature as essential values, that commits to the joy of "living well" and the "good life," rather than the complacent, egotistical "well-being" that the market sells us, and which ends up isolating us and enclosing us in our little worlds.

They called for dignified work and housing, and access to land for smallholders; for integrating poor urban neighborhoods into the life of the city; for curbing discrimination and violence against women; for stopping all forms of slavery; for ending war, organized crime, and repression; for shoring up democratic freedom of expression and communication; and for ensuring that science and technology serve the people.

None of these can happen without change in every community, which in turn can only happen through concrete actions in which all are protagonists and that flow from seeing, judging, and acting: sensing need, discerning which way to go, and building consensus for action.

There will be temptations that distract us: to chew on a sense of powerlessness and anger; to remain stuck in conflicts and grievances; to focus on slogans and abstract ideas rather than specific, local actions. And let's not be naive: there will always be the danger of corruption. That is why, to join the cause and the style of the people's movements you need humility and some personal austerity; this is a path of service, not a route to power. So if you have a penchant for fine dining and luxury cars and other such things, stay away from the people's movements and from politics (and, please, from the seminary, too). A sober, humble lifestyle dedicated to service is worth far more than thousands of followers on social networks.

Our greatest power is not in the respect that others have for us, but the service we can offer others. In every action we carry out for the sake of others we lay the foundations for restoring the dignity of our peoples and communities, and in so doing allow us to better heal, care, and share. While these actions need to involve all of us, there is much that political and business leaders can do to facilitate these priorities, which are nothing less than the needs of the people they belong to.

To help us envision this better future, we can think of those three Ls which the Popular Movements promote. If we put land as well as decent lodging and labor for all at the center of our actions, we will be able to create a virtuous cycle that over time helps us to restore the dignity of our peoples.

LAND

We are earthly beings, who belong to Mother Earth, and we cannot simply live at her expense; our relationship with her is reciprocal. We need now a Jubilee, a time when those who have more than enough should consume less to allow the earth to heal, and a time for the excluded to find their place in our societies. The pandemic and the economic crisis offer a chance to examine our lifestyles, to change destructive habits, and to find more sustainable ways to produce, trade, and transport goods.

We can also begin to implement an ecological conversion at every level of society in the ways that I suggested in *Laudato Si'*: moving to renewable energy and away from fossil fuels; respecting and implementing biodiversity; guaranteeing access to clean water; adopting more restrained lifestyles; changing our understanding of value, progress, and success by taking into account the impact of our businesses on the environment.

As a world community we must commit to meet the United Nations' sustainable development goals by 2030. Let us use the years ahead to practice an *integral* ecology, allowing the principle of ecological regeneration to shape the decisions we take at every level.

This means taking a long, hard look at the impact of our industrial methods on the environment and of agribusiness on small farmers. More land needs to be opened up to smallholders growing food for local consumption using organic, sustainable methods. Our farms need to produce not just food but healthy soil and biodiversity.

The goods and resources of the earth are meant for all. Fresh air, clean water, and a balanced diet are vital for the health and well-being of our peoples. Let us put the regeneration of the earth and universal access to its goods at the heart of our post-Covid future.

LODGING

By "lodging" I obviously mean the homes we live in, but in a broader sense our general habitat.

With an ever greater concentration of people in cities, what happens there will be key to the future of our civilization. It is hard to be conscious of our dignity as a people when we are sunk in soulless city centers, without history. It is hard to speak of belonging and shared responsibility

170

when we think of huge urban sprawls that foster anonymity, solitude, and a sense of orphanhood. The degradation of our urban environment is a sign of cultural exhaustion. When our surroundings are chaotic, fragmented, and saturated with noise and ugliness, it is hard to be happy or to speak of dignity.

To restore the dignity of our peoples means attending to our *oikos*—that is, to our common home. There is so much to be done to humanize our urban environment: creating, encouraging, and caring for common areas and green spaces, ensuring dignified, sustainable, family-friendly housing for all, developing neighborhoods and quality public transport networks to reduce pollution and noise that also enable people to move around quickly and safely. We must dignify the peripheral areas of our cities, integrating them by means of social policies that recognize and value the cultural contribution that they can make. Transforming our cities in this way generates social and cultural wealth that makes possible and encourages care for the environment.

But all these efforts must be led by local agents, from within their culture, supported by the state of course, but with respect, always, for the voice and actions of those who live in the place and their institutions. The goal must be to enable networks of belonging and solidarity to flourish by restoring the bonds of community and fraternity, engaging institutions rooted in the community together with people's movements. When organizations act together beyond boundaries of belief and ethnicity to achieve concrete goals for their communities, then we can say that our peoples have claimed back their soul.

LABOR

God gave us the land to till and keep. Our work is the basic condition of our dignity and well-being. Labor is not the exclusive privilege of the employed or the employers but a right and duty for all men and women.

What will our future look like when 40 or 50 percent of young people are jobless, as is the case now in some countries? People might need particular assistance for a time but should not need to live on welfare. They need to earn a dignified living through their labor, in the first place to support their families and develop themselves, but also to enrich their surroundings and communities. Work is the capacity that the Lord gifted us with that lets us contribute to His creative action. In working, we shape creation.

That is why, as a society, we have to ensure that labor be a means not just of earning money but of self-expression, of taking part in society, and of contributing to the common good. Prioritizing access to work must become a core goal of national public policies.

Many words in the business world suggest the fraternal purpose of economic activity we must now reestablish: "company," for example, comes from sharing bread together, while "corporation" means integration into the body. Business isn't just a private enterprise; it should serve the "common" good. Common comes from the Latin *cum-munus*: "cum" means together, while "munus" has the meaning of a service given as a gift or out of a sense of duty. Our work has both an individual and a common dimension. It is a source of personal growth as well as being key to restoring the dignity of our peoples.

Too often we have it the wrong way around: despite the fact that they create value, workers are treated as the most expendable element of an enterprise, while some shareholders—with their narrow interest in maximizing profits—call the shots. Our definition of the value of work is also far too narrow. We need to move beyond this idea that the work of the caregiver for her relative, or a full-time mother or volunteer in a social project, is not work because it pays no wages.

Recognizing the value to society of the work of nonearners is a vital part of our rethinking in the post-Covid world. That's why I believe it is time to explore concepts like the universal basic income (UBI), also known as "the negative income tax": an unconditional flat payment to all citizens, which could be dispersed through the tax system.

The UBI could reshape relations in the labor market, guaranteeing people the dignity of refusing employment terms that trap them in poverty. It would give people the basic security they need, remove the stigma of welfarism, and make it easier to move between jobs as technology-driven labor patterns increasingly demand. Policies like the UBI can also help free people to combine earning wages with giving time to the community.

With the same objective, it may well be time to consider reduced working hours with adjusted salaries, which can paradoxically increase productivity. Working less so that more people can gain access to the labor market is one aspect of the kind of thinking we urgently need to explore.

By making the integration of the poor and the care for our environment central to society's goals, we can generate work while humanizing our surroundings. By providing a universal basic income, we can free and enable people to work for the community in a dignified way. By adopting more intensive permaculture methods for growing food, we can regenerate the natural world, create work and biodiversity, and live better.

All this means having common-good goals for human development rather than the false assumption of the infamous trickle-down theory that a growing economy will make us all richer. By focusing on land, lodging, and labor we can regain a healthy relationship with the world and grow by serving others.

In this way, we transcend the narrow individualist framework of the liberal paradigm without falling into the trap of populism. Democracy is then reinvigorated by the concerns and wisdom of the people who are involved in it. Politics can once again be an expression of love through service. By making the restoration of our peoples' dignity the central objective of the post-Covid world, we make everyone's dignity the key to our actions. To guarantee a world where dignity is valued and respected through concrete actions is not just a dream but a path to a better future.

Epilogue

We might wonder: And now what must I do? What could be my place in this future, and what can I do to make it possible?

Two words come to mind: "decenter" and "transcend."

See where you are centered, and decenter yourself. The task is to open doors and windows, and move out beyond. Remember what I said at the start about the risk of getting bogged down in the same patterns of thinking and acting. What we must avoid is the temptation to center on ourselves.

A crisis forces you to move, but one can move without going anywhere. In lockdown many of us left the house or apartment to shop for essentials or walk around the block to stretch our legs. But then we went back to where and what we were before, like a tourist who goes to the sea or the mountains for a week of relaxation but then returns to her suffocating routine. She has moved, but sideways, only to come back to where she started.

I prefer the contrasting image of the pilgrim, who is one who decenters and so can transcend. She goes out from herself, opens herself to a new horizon, and when she comes home she is no longer the same, and so her home won't be the same.

This is a time for pilgrimages.

There is a kind of walking ahead which just puts you ever deeper inside your shell, like the labyrinth of Greek myth which Theseus enters.

A labyrinth doesn't have to be just a physical space where we go around and around; we can create a labyrinth out of the future in our minds. Jorge Luis Borges has a short story, "The Garden of Forking Paths," about a novel in which diverse futures and outcomes are all possible, each leading to another one, where nothing is ever resolved because nothing excludes anything else. It is a nightmare, because there is no real possibility of a way out.

You come out of a labyrinth only in two ways: either by going up, decentering and transcending, or by allowing yourself to be led out by Ariadne's thread.

The labyrinth is where the world is right now, and we're going around and around, trying not to get eaten by various "Minotaurs"; or we're moving ahead but along forking paths of endless possibilities that never get us to where we need to be.

The labyrinth might be our assumption that life will go back to "normal." It might reflect our egotism, our individualism, our not-seeing, our wanting things to go back to how they were, ignoring the fact that we weren't so fine before.

In the Greek myth, Ariadne hands Theseus a ball of thread to track his way out. The ball of thread we have been given is our creativity to move beyond the logic of the labyrinth, to decenter and transcend. Ariadne's gift is the Spirit calling us out of ourselves—the "twitch upon the thread" of which G. K. Chesterton spoke in his Father Brown stories. It is others who, like Ariadne, help us to find a way out, to give the best of ourselves.

The worst thing that can happen to us is that we stay behind, looking in the mirror, dizzy from so much spinning around without an exit. To get out of the labyrinth we have to leave behind the "selfie" culture and look at the eyes, faces, hands, and needs of those around us; and in this way find, too, our own faces, our own hands full of possibilities.

Once we feel that "twitch upon the thread" there are many ways to emerge from the labyrinth. What they have in common is the realization that we belong to each other in a mutual relationship, that we are part of a people, and that our destiny is a shared one. "Certainly the most decisive turning points in world history are substantially co-determined by souls whom no history book ever mentions," wrote Edith Stein (Saint Teresa Benedicta of the Cross). "And we will only find out about those souls to whom we owe the decisive turning points in our personal lives on the day when all that is hidden is revealed."[31] They are the ones able to pull on our thread.

Let yourself be pulled along, shaken up, challenged. Maybe it'll be through something you've read in these pages; maybe through a group of people you've heard about on the news, or that you know about in your neighborhood, whose story has moved you. Perhaps it'll be a local elderly people's home or refugee hospitality center or ecological regeneration project that is calling to you. Or maybe people closer to home who need you.

When you feel the twitch, stop and pray. Read the Gospel, if you're a Christian. Or just create space inside yourself to listen. Open yourself . . . decenter . . . transcend.

And then act. Call up, go visit, offer your service. Say you don't have a clue what they do, but maybe you can help. Say you'd like to be part of a different world, and you thought this might be a good place to start.

I'd like to end with a poem that I read in lockdown after receiving it from a friend in Argentina. There was some confusion over the author, who I eventually found out is a Cuban actor and comedian in Miami. When I spoke on the phone with Alexis Valdés, he told me he wrote "Hope" ("Esperanza") in a single sitting, without changing the words, as if God had used him as a channel. It went viral, moving many—including me. It captures the path to the better future I have tried to express in this book. Let's let his poetry and its beauty have the final word, helping us to decenter and transcend so that our peoples may have life (John 10:10).

HOPE

When the storm has passed
and the roads are tamed
and we are the survivors
of a collective shipwreck.

With tearful heart
and our destiny blessed
we will feel joy
simply for being alive.

And we'll give a hug
to the first stranger
and praise our good luck
that we kept a friend.

And then we'll remember
all that we lost
and finally learn
everything we never learned.

And we'll envy no one
for all of us have suffered
and we'll not be idle
but more compassionate.

We'll value more what belongs to all
than what was earned.
We'll be more generous
and much more committed.

We'll understand how fragile
it is to be alive.
We'll sweat empathy
for those still with us and those who are gone.

We'll miss the old man
who asked for a buck in the market
whose name we never knew
who was always at your side.

And maybe the poor old man
was your God in disguise.
But you never asked his name
because you never had the time.

And all will become a miracle.
And all will become a legacy.
And we'll respect the life,
the life we have gained.

When the storm passes
I ask you Lord, in shame
that you return us better,
as you once dreamed us.[32]

Postscript by Austen Ivereigh

Let Us Dream was born in lockdown, specifically in that moment when Pope Francis appeared in Saint Peter's Square like a storm pilot to guide humanity through one of its darkest nights.

It was on March 27, 2020, a fortnight before that uneasy Easter of empty churches and deserted streets, when from the dark, rainy, abandoned square he gave a powerful, unscheduled "Urbi et Orbi" reflection. Watched by millions on their TVs and tablets, Francis made clear that the world faced a turning point, a time of trial, from which we could either come out better or slide sharply backward.

Shortly after, the Pope shared with me in a fascinating eve-of-Easter interview some of his insights on the temptations, obstacles, and opportunities that the crisis presented. As so often with Francis, the ideas came as flashes of intuition that left me restless to know more. Then, just after Easter, it was announced that Francis had appointed a Vatican commission to consult experts across the world on the post-Covid future. The Pope asked the commission to "prepare the future": he saw the Church not just responding to what was to come, but helping to shape it. Outwardly the "Pope in lockdown," cut off from the people, looked helpless. Yet those close to him told me the opposite: that he was energized by what he saw as a threshold moment, and the movement of spirits beneath its surface.

I seized the moment to suggest a book that would give him the space to develop his thoughts and make them available to a broader public. Amazingly, he agreed, while making clear he would need more from me than a series of questions. As was clear from his daily homilies broadcast from his residence during lockdown, he had a lot to say in depth and a question-answer format would not be enough.

In his response to the crisis, Francis wasn't simply serving up diagnoses and prescriptions. What concerned him was the process of transformation itself: how historic change happens, how we resist or embrace that process: the dynamic of conversion. As I knew from researching his life, this was—among his many gifts—his particular charism, forged in decades of spiritual leadership in his native Argentina that now as Pope he was drawing on to walk with humanity. Francis was, to coin a phrase, the world's spiritual director; and now that the world had entered a dark night, he was walking with us, shining a torch onto the paths ahead and warning us off the cliff edges. He sought to communicate the urgency of opening the people to the grace that was always on offer in times of tribulation, and so let God shape our story.

I suggested a three-part narrative that could capture that process of conversion. The see-judge-act method has been used often by the Latin American Church to respond to change. Francis had reformulated it in different terms ("contemplate-discern-propose") but it was essentially the same approach. First, look at reality, however uncomfortable, above all the truth of the suffering in the margins of society. Second, discern the different forces at work, distinguishing what builds up from what destroys, what humanizes from what dehumanizes, and thus choose what is of God, rejecting the opposite. Finally, propose fresh thinking and concrete steps that stem from the diagnosis of what ails us and how we might act differently. This is the basic structure of *Let Us Dream*, divided into three "times": to see, to choose, and to act.

In the course of exchanges with Francis between June and August 2020, I invited him to go deeply into two related areas of his thinking on unity in action that have been in many ways his life project and the key to his spiritual leadership.

One was the question of how we forge unity from tension, holding together differences to make them fruitful rather than letting them fall into contradiction. This is the dynamic at the heart of the synodal processes he has put into place in the Church, which humanity urgently needs at this time. The other was about the catalyzing effect of the awareness of being God's people, and how a people organizes on the basis of that awareness. Francis is convinced, as these pages show, that true change comes about not from above but from the margins where Christ lives. Behind this conviction is the rich tradition of reflection by the Argentine Church known as the Theology of the People.

Both of these topics, central to his papacy, have been widely misunderstood; both topics are essential for coming out of this crisis.

Initially I asked questions and he recorded his thoughts; Part One is the fruit of those exchanges. But as the book developed, it became more of a master-disciple collaboration: he would send me references and journal articles, make suggestions, and give me ideas to develop. *Let Us Dream* emerged organically, from these exchanges, followed by his revisions and suggestions, allowing us to create two texts: one that sounded natural in my native English, the other in his Spanish, using his own phrases and patterns of speech characteristic of the people of Buenos Aires. We finished just as Francis resumed his meetings, and people began returning to the Square. A new era of the crisis was starting, more complex than lockdown.

In his messages to me in signoffs at the end of recordings Francis was full of energy, passion, and humor. But I could feel the intensity with which he was living this time: how he suffered with others, and his sense of urgency. He was unfailingly tender and encouraging, becoming intensely involved in the revision process to bring us to the finish line. I shall always be deeply grateful to him for his trust.

I would also like to thank Fathers Diego Fares and Augusto Zampini-Davies for their support and contributions; Julia Torres in Rome and María Galli-Terra in Montevideo for help synchronizing the Spanish edition; and Alexis Valdés for the use of his famous poem. I owe much to Eamon Dolan's team at Simon & Schuster, who heroically expedited a high-speed operation at an extremely difficult time for the publishing world. Thanks as always to Stephen Rubin, who is more than a publisher, and to Bill Barry, who is more than a literary agent; to my wife, Linda, for enduring patiently and sustaining magnificently; and to the Virgin Mary, "Untier of Knots," for help when it was most needed.

Notes

Endnotes prepared by Austen Ivereigh

1. Friedrich Hölderlin. *Sämtliche Werke*, Stuttgarter Ausgabe, Vol. 2, Parte 1, S. 165 (Stuttgart, 1951).
2. In April 2016 Pope Francis visited Lesbos in the company of two Orthodox Church leaders: His Holiness Bartholomew, Ecumenical Patriarch of Constantinople, and His Beatitude Ieronymos, Archbishop of Athens and of All Greece. He returned to Rome with twelve Muslim refugees.
3. The meeting of 190 world leaders in Paris was known as "COP21" because it was the twenty-first yearly session of the "Conference of Parties" to the 1992 United Nations Framework Convention on Climate Change. The Paris agreement to limit the increase in global temperature in this century to 1.5 degrees Celsius was a historic achievement which many afterwards attributed in part to the influence of *Laudato Si'* and the efforts of Pope Francis. See Austen Ivereigh, *Wounded Shepherd: Pope Francis and His Struggle to Convert the Catholic Church* (New York: Henry Holt, 2019), 216–18.

4. *Morals on the Book of Job* by St. Gregory the Great, ed. Paul A. Böer, Sr., anonymously translated (Veritatis Splendor Publications, 2012), Book 10, Number 47.
5. Pope Francis here refers to a period (1990–1992) he spent in the mountain city of Córdoba in central Argentina. It came at the end of a turbulent period in the Argentine province of the Society of Jesus following more than a decade of Jorge Mario Bergoglio as its dominant, charismatic leader, both as provincial (1973–1979) and rector of the Jesuit formation house, the Colegio Máximo in Buenos Aires province. At this point only in his mid-fifties, Bergoglio was sent to Córdoba. The period came to an end when the then Archbishop of Buenos Aires, Cardinal Antonio Quarracino, asked Pope John Paul II to name him his auxiliary (assistant) bishop. This painful but fruitful period, when Jorge Mario Bergoglio suffered greatly and wrote some of his most profound insights, is described in Austen Ivereigh, *The Great Reformer: Francis and the Making of a Radical Pope* (New York: Henry Holt/ Picador, 2014/2015), chapter 5.
6. In his *Spiritual Exercises*, the founder of the Jesuits, Saint Ignatius of Loyola, notes (332) how "it is characteristic of the bad angel to assume the form of an angel of light. . . . That

is to say, he proposes good and holy thoughts well adapted to such a just soul, and then succeeds little by little in getting his own way, drawing the soul into his hidden snares and perverted purposes." *The Spiritual Exercises of Saint Ignatius of Loyola*, trans. Michael Ivens, SJ (Leominster, UK: Gracewing, 2004), p. 100.

7. *Ut annis consolidetur, dilatetur tempore, sublimetur aetate* is a famous formula of Saint Vincent of Lérins, died c. 450, who was chief theologian of the Abbey of Lérins in France.

8. Francisco Luis Bernárdez, "Soneto," from *Cielo de tierra* (Earth Sky), 1937.

9. Kate Raworth, *Doughnut Economics: 7 Ways to Think Like a 21st-Century Economist* (London: Penguin Random House, 2017), and Mariana Mazzucato, *The Value of Everything: Making & Taking in the Global Economy* (London: Penguin Random House, 2019), are among five female economists described as "revolutionizing their field" in an article in *Forbes* magazine. See Avivah Wittenberg-Cox, "5 Economists Redefining . . . Everything. Oh Yes, and They're Women," *Forbes* (forbes.com), May 31, 2020. Another influential economist, Professor (Sister) Alessandra Smerilli, is a member of the Vatican's post-Covid commission.

10. All Vatican dicasteries (as its departments are known) have consultants appointed by the Pope. They meet regularly in Rome to advise and give input, bringing outside perspectives to the process of decision-making. Francis is the first Pope, for example, to have named three women consultants to the Congregation for the Doctrine of the Faith, and two to the Congregation for Divine Worship and the Discipline of the Sacraments, making it possible for women to be heard in two of the most important Vatican bodies, responsible for doctrine and liturgy.

11. Pope Francis here refers to the section of the Secretariat of State which acts as the equivalent of a State Department or Foreign Ministry under the secretary for relations with states. Two undersecretaries answer to the secretary: one oversees the work of the Church's diplomats, the other coordinates relations with multilateral organizations. Francesca Di Giovanni is the first woman to hold the latter post.

12. Pope Francis's encylical, *Fratelli Tutti* ("Brothers and Sisters All"), was signed on October 3, 2020.

13. The term "isolated conscience" appears in the first sentence of #2 in *Evangelii Gaudium* (*The Joy of the Gospel*), Francis's first major document as Pope. (In the Vatican's English

translation it is wrongly rendered as "blunted conscience.")

14. "Acquired fortune" (*cosa adquisita*) appears in #150 of the *Spiritual Exercises* of Saint Ignatius of Loyola. The exercise known as "three classes" helps people to recognize unconscious mechanisms of self-justification that restrict spiritual freedom. Saint Ignatius imagines three people who "have each acquired 10,000 ducats, but not purely and as would have been right for the love of God. They all want to be saved and to find God our Lord in peace by getting rid of the burden and obstacle to this purpose contained in their attachment to the acquired fortune."

15. Saint Dorotheus of Gaza, "Sobre la acusación de sí mismo," no. 100, in Jorge Mario Bergoglio, *Reflexiones espirituales sobre la vida apostólica* (Bilbao: Mensajero, 2013), p. 137.

16. "Visit to the Joint Session of the United States Congress: 'Address of the Holy Father,' " U.S. Capitol, Washington, D.C., September 24, 2015.

17. The German priest, writer, and academic Romano Guardini (1885–1968) was one of the most influential Catholic thinkers of the twentieth century. Pope Francis's unfinished thesis focused on an early (1925) work of philosophical anthropology of Guardini's that

has never been translated into English. *Der Gegensatz: Versuche zu einer Philosophie des Lebendig-Konkreten* was published in Spanish as *El Contraste: Ensayo de una filosofía de lo viviente-concreto*, trans. Alfonso López Quintas (Madrid: Biblioteca de Autores Cristianos, 1996). Jorge Mario Bergoglio's thesis was titled "Polar Opposition as Structure of Daily Thought and of Christian Proclamation." He revealed this to Massimo Borghesi, whose *The Mind of Pope Francis: Jorge Mario Bergoglio's Intellectual Journey* (Collegeville, Minn.: Liturgical Press, 2017) describes the thesis in detail in chapter 3.

18. When the Synod of Bishops meets again in Rome in October 2022, it will be on the theme "For a Synodal Church: Communion, Participation and Mission."

19. In the 1964 "Constitution on the Church," known as *Lumen Gentium* ("Light of the People") #12, the Second Vatican Council decreed: "The entire body of the faithful, anointed as they are by the Holy One, cannot err in matters of belief. They manifest this special property by means of the whole peoples' supernatural discernment in matters of faith when 'from the Bishops down to the last of the lay faithful' they show universal agreement in matters of faith and morals."

20. The maxim, in use for many centuries in different forms, appears in the attempt to codify Church law under Boniface VIII (1294–1303) as *Quod omnes tangit debet ab omnibus approbari.* In the American Revolution, "No taxation without representation" expressed a similar idea.

21. *Amoris Laetitia*, chapter 8, titled "Accompanying, Discerning, and Integrating Weakness," lays out an approach for how the Church should care for the divorced and remarried, integrating them into parish life, and helping them see how God is calling them. For a detailed account of the Synod on the Family, including its eleventh-hour resolution and Pope Francis's post-synod document, see Ivereigh, *Wounded Shepherd*, chapters 9 and 10.

22. In the Catholic Church a deacon is an ordained member of the clergy but not a priest. Deacons can lead marriage services, preside at funerals, and perform baptisms, but cannot hear confessions or celebrate the Eucharist. The diaconate is either a stage toward priesthood ("transitional deacons") or, as here, "permanent." Normally a "permanent deacon" is married with a family, and, unlike a priest, who is moved around by his bishop, will be tied to a particular community, where he will often be very

involved in caring for the poor and visiting the housebound. Pope Francis is pointing here to this local focus of the permanent diaconate as a gift to Amazonia, which in his view is yet to be properly embraced by the Church in the area.

23. Poem 63 in *Gitanjali* (London: Macmillan, 1918).
24. Fyodor Dostoyevsky, *The Brothers Kara-mazov*, Part II, Book VI, chapter III.
25. The universal destination of goods is the principle of social Catholic teaching that God intends the goods of the earth for all, without distinction. This principle does not contradict the right of private property, but relativizes it. Ownership brings with it obligations to the common good.
26. Francis, "Meeting with Priests, Consecrated Men and Women, and Seminarians," Santiago Cathedral (January 16, 2018).
27. "Visit to the Joint Session of the United States Congress: 'Address of the Holy Father,'" U.S. Capitol, Washington, D.C., September 24, 2015.
28. According to World Health Organization figures.
29. Or in Latin: *Terra, Domus, Labor*. See Guzmán Carriquiry Lecour and Gianni La Bella, *La irrupción de los movimientos populares: "Rerum Novarum" de nuesto*

tiempo, preface by Pope Francis (Libreria Editrice Vaticana, 2019).

30. "To an Invisible Army. Letter to the Popular Movements, April 12, 2020," in Pope Francis, *Life After the Pandemic*, preface by Cardinal Michael Czerny SJ (Libreria Editrice Vaticana, 2020), pp. 35–40.

31. *Verborgenes Leben und Epiphanie*: GW XI, 145.

32. Alexis Valdés, "Esperanza" (2020). English translation by América Valdés, Nilo Cruz, and Alexis Valdés for *Let Us Dream*.

About the Authors

Jorge Mario Bergoglio was born in Buenos Aires, Argentina, on December 17, 1936, the son of Italian immigrants. He was ordained a priest in the Society of Jesus (Jesuits) in 1969, named Provincial in 1973, and rector of the Colegio Máximo in Buenos Aires in 1980. He was consecrated bishop in 1992, became Archbishop of Buenos Aires in 1998, and was appointed a cardinal in 2001. In March 2013 he was elected Bishop of Rome, the 266th pope of the Catholic Church.

Dr. Austen Ivereigh, a British writer and journalist, is the author of two biographies of Pope Francis: *The Great Reformer* (2014) and *Wounded Shepherd* (2019). He is Fellow in Contemporary Church History at Campion Hall, University of Oxford.

Mindful of Pope Francis's call in *Let Us Dream* to care for creation, the authors will offset the CO_2 emissions associated with the first printing of the hardcover edition of the book in the United States. Through Natural Capital Partners, they have purchased offsets from a water filtration and improved cookstove project in Guatemala, which reduces emissions by avoiding deforestation and also contributes to ten of the UN's Sustainable Development Goals.

Books are produced in the United States using U.S.-based materials

Books are printed using a revolutionary new process called THINKtech™ that lowers energy usage by 70% and increases overall quality

Books are durable and flexible because of Smyth-sewing

Paper is sourced using environmentally responsible foresting methods and the paper is acid-free

Center Point Large Print
600 Brooks Road / PO Box 1
Thorndike, ME 04986-0001 USA

(207) 568-3717

US & Canada:
1 800 929-9108
www.centerpointlargeprint.com